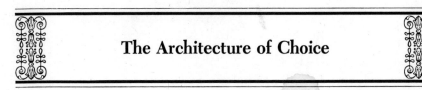

The Architecture of Choice

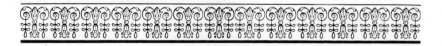

BY THE SAME AUTHOR:

Historic Buildings of Ohio

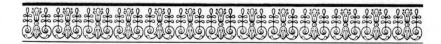

The ARCHITECTURE of Choice:

ECLECTICISM IN AMERICA 1880-1930

Walter C. Kidney

GEORGE BRAZILLER   *New York*

For information address the publisher:
George Braziller, Inc., One Park Avenue, New York, N.Y. 10016

Library of Congress Catalog Number: 73-88044
Standard Book Number: 0-8076-0730-4, cloth
                       0-8076-0731-2, paper

Printed in the U.S.A.

DESIGNED BY RONALD FARBER

Lithographed by The Murray Printing Company

Acknowledgments

PETER GREEN, for pointing out that as long as I was writing a book I might
as well find a publisher; JOHN MAASS, for suggesting the title; CHARLOTTE
LARUE, of the Museum of the City of New York, for her helpfulness in finding
pictures; ADOLF PLACZEK and the staff of the Avery Library, for help of
various kinds; NORRIS HOYT, of St. George's School, Newport, for giving the
chapel as a photography class assignment; THEODORE BOWMAN, architect of
the University of Pittsburgh, for telling me about the Cathedral of Learning
and getting me pictures; WILLIAM SEALE, for help and advice in getting
pictures of state capitols; EDWARD TEITELMAN, for information on Philadelphia
buildings.

Contents

Preface

This short book can cover only the surface of its subject: trace the history of Eclecticism, mention a few names, suggest some of the topics that need further investigation, and offer a few opinions. Even so, perhaps it will help to stimulate interest in a subject that is beginning to attract serious attention once again.

Eclecticism ceased to have any intellectual respectability some time around 1930, when it was often denounced, to intellectuals, as a mere bad habit that needed breaking. For critics since that time it has seemed too spiritually supine and too corrupted by noncultural considerations to be worth bothering with, and for art historians it has been too recent and perhaps—since "modern" art has dominated the respectable critical media—too eccentric, too unpopular. Here, however, a "silent majority" paradox is at work, for many, by no means brainless, people have remained perfectly happy with Eclectic architecture in their homes, churches, and places of business over the last four decades. Just as a priest of the Baroque period might feel an affection for his outmoded Gothic church and a family of 1920 be fond of its ugly mansardic house of 1870, so many more recent individuals have found a sympathetic environment for home life, worship, and work in the Tudor of 1915 and the Neo-Georgian of 1925. The purpose of this book, then, is not only to trace the history of Eclecticism but to attempt to give those whose cultural attitude includes a rejection of it a sense of the ideas related to Eclecticism and the qualities of the architecture it produced.

For the sake of simplicity I have divided American architecture since 1870 into four categories:

Mid-Victorian architecture, dominant in 1870 but soon to decline—imitative of historic styles but only loosely, without regard for correctness of proportion, scale, or materials;

Aesthetic architecture, introduced in the early 1870s as part of an English-inspired reform in the decorative arts—using historic decorative motifs freely for picturesque effect, without regard to correctness, and showing a renewed interest in refinements of form, color, and texture;

Eclecticism, beginning, in my opinion, in 1874 and in decline since 1930—learnedly if selectively imitative of historic architecture in all aspects of its appearance, and using the historic styles as expressions of various cultural institutions;

Modernism, evolving from various sources including the Aesthetic Movement, and dominant today—having many philosophies, many kinds of approach to form and materials, but tenuously unified by abstention from the historic styles.

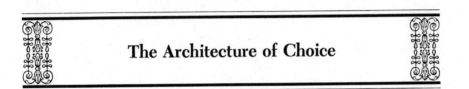

The Architecture of Choice

What Was Eclecticism?

Imagine a well-to-do American businessman, motoring home some time around 1928. Pausing before a Tudor archway, stone in stucco, he opens garage doors of a standard pattern, then drives his car into a space lined with terra-cotta block and lighted with a single naked bulb. He walks up two steps into a kitchen area of cream-painted nonarchitecture, then into a rather diminutive great hall, with diamond-paned windows, massive beams of varnished boards, and a baronial fireplace of painted cement; then up the stairs to a bathroom of tile and porcelain and nickel plating. No sense of incongruity or shock for our businessman in his passage from space to space, no feeling that something of the great hall need be brought into the bathroom or, for that matter, that the bathroom should dictate to the great hall: each of them he finds good in its way and in its place, and indeed he is proud of both. At his ease in the great hall later, a glass of best Prohibition Scotch at his fingertips, his reading eye may fall upon a manifesto calling for a new architecture: "We can no longer . . . ; we must . . . " If so—actually, it is not very likely that he would—he will probably look up, and about, and sneer, "*Who* must?" Millions in 1928 would have said the same (Fig. 1).

If Eclecticism has been without intellectual respectability in the last forty years, it is partly because it never was very intellectual. The various strains of modernism that pushed it into the background were impelled on a tide of words, of rebukes and demands and invocations of democracy, nature, honesty, the zeitgeist, The Machine, science, mathematics, and other matters whose newly assigned role as arbiters of architectural form needed some explaining. The Eclectics were less cerebral. One may perhaps generalize about the Eclectic classicists, Gothicists, and the others and describe their art as an affair of taking up forms of proven and mature beauty from the formal and the vernacular architectures of the past and adapting them, learnedly but with personal touches, to modern building programs. Everyone was familiar with the forms in question; well handled by an architect of talent, they had a beauty that needed no explanation, no philosophy. Nor—for a while at least—was there much question of their appropriateness in modern America: not as long as they were faithful to the prevailing sense of cultural context.

Not only were the forms of historic architecture valuable through their beauty, but they came to our times freighted with historic associations that every cultured person was familiar with, and that seemed to suggest, even to demand, that a certain building, in a certain place, be built in some one of a rather restricted range of styles. Because the first high-style architecture of British America was Colonial and later "Early Republican," these styles were acceptable in just about any building where their modest scale was not overstrained. In Florida and California, where the Spanish past was romanticized, the full range of Spanish, or at least of Mediterranean, styles was equally common. In the Southwest, a Pueblo style flourished for a while, and in the New Orleans area a Creole. Parts of the country where the earliest buildings were mid-Victorian —and thus in deep disgrace—tended to choose architectural styles under the other, more universal and even more important, aspect of cultural context: the historic background of the building type. When style was thus determined, a house was usually Georgian, Tudor, or Cotswold (Anglo-Saxon home atmosphere), unless it was a mansion and intended to look like one, in which case it might have been Jacobean or one of the Louis (aristocracy of wealth). A church —if not Colonial—would, for an old and ritualistic sect, be Gothic (Christian heritage); if it was for some new sect, like the Christian Scientists, it might be decently but noncommittally wrapped in something classical. A synagogue, in the absence of a true Hebraic architecture, was usually Byzantine or Moorish (Fig. 2). A school was Tudor or Jacobean (Oxford, Eton). A theater was either Louis XV (courtly diversions) or—especially if a movie house— something utterly fantastic, with some sort of high-pressure Mediterranean Baroque providing the norm (palace of illusions). For the center city, classicism was long the near-universal solution; a cluster of styles, rather than a single style, it clothed the museum, the library, the memorial structure in cool eternal beauty, but broke into rustications, ressauts, and swags, giant orders and Renaissance cornices for the more worldly office buildings, the bank, the apartment house, the theater, the clubhouse, and the town mansion (Figs. 3, 4). It had manners for both the places of contemplation and secular solemnity and the places of sociability and business. Certain modern problems, though, were too much even for classicism; the post-1916 skyscraper in New York and the architecture of transportation seemed to call urgently for something new; this the Eclectics, after the early 1920s, began to supply.

And not with much regret. One senses that, even without forceful opposition and economic catastrophe, Eclectic architects would not have kept on designing in the historic styles forever. Around 1925, there seems to have been an understanding that although the traditional building types—the house, the school, and the church—would continue indefinitely in the styles associated with them by that time, the skyscraper, the engineering work, the powerhouse, the smart shop, and in fact all the places where a venturesome up-to-dateness was not a bad thing to emphasize or where the demands of the building program could make the older styles look a little silly might be in some new idiom, some variety perhaps of Art Deco or Modernistic. The line of demarcation would doubtless advance further into the traditional territory in time, slowly, cautiously.

The amount and kind of imitativeness among the Eclectics varied from architect to architect and decade to decade. Literal imitation did occur: the tower of Independence Hall has a way of turning up here and there, as do the dome of St. Peter's, the Trianons, and the porch of Compton Wynyates (Fig. 5).[1] But such copies or near-copies are exceptional. The Eclectic saw himself as a participant in, or an heir to, a reform movement that had restored taste and literacy to architecture (Fig. 6).[2] Unlike the mid-Victorian, the Eclectic studied all aspects of the style in which he proposed to design not just the standard ornamental motifs, but the scale, proportions, massing, colors, and textures. These things contributed, in varying degrees, to the true look of the style. Once his contribution was assessed, the Eclectic felt free to introduce variations of his own: to abbreviate or suppress typical ornamental details, even to create original ones; to substitute a new material for an "authentic" one. By a skillful adjustment of the elements and by careful detailing he could create something marginally original, yet free of any feeling of incongruity, relying on his sense of how the style of choice worked visually. As Cram did in many of his churches, or McKim in the Low Library at Columbia, he could synthesize several styles, or, like Goodhue at the end of his life, build out from the historic styles to attempt new ones.

The ways in which the Eclectics used their literacy differed throughout the period—indeed, a glance is often enough to tell, within ten years, when an Eclectic building was designed. In the

1890s, the architecture was usually "too" broad and bulky, and its decorative elements seem to have been assembled around the bare shell of the building rather than conceived as harmonious modifications of it. Later, the elements were more skillfully integrated, more correctly proportioned and detailed, but toward 1920 the literacy threatened to become literalism. At the same time, the past was edited. Everything became overly mellow, recreated history seen in soft focus, with all the harshnesses of historic architecture refined away, the colors muted, the surfaces softened. High-quality materials and workmanship could redeem the design from insipidity; after 1930 these were not to be relied upon. But even as the technique of the Eclectic as a student of the Styles threatened to become too perfect, the forces that turned him toward modernism were at work, and by 1925 intelligent architects and critics began to wonder what was going to happen next.

Indeed, though the rich home builder may have wanted to buy an illusion of Quattrocento Tuscany or Versailles, or some Ludwig II fantasy to comfort his hungry ego, and though the architect himself may have had his imaginary unspoiled towns, clinging to Italian hillsides or reflected in the Tigris, the profession was always at pains to assert the relevance, the appropriateness, of its work to the United States of 1915 or 1925, to prove that, even though the styles might be historical, the works themselves were vital and in the spirit of a living tradition.[3]

The Nightmare of the Eclectics

Looking back on American architecture in 1870, the Eclectic of the 1920s was inclined to shudder (Fig. 7).[4] Though he conceded that Upjohn and Renwick had been real architects, and that the simplest examples of the Italian Villa style of the 1850s showed a certain low order of taste, this was as much as he was prepared to admit. For the rest, he leveled at mid-Victorian architecture much the same charges that the modernists were about to direct against him—charges of philistinism, perversion of values, commercialism. He saw in the architecture of 1870 a nightmare version of the real thing—mansard roofs, brownstone fronts, raw red brick laced with cold white marble, the Renaissance in cast iron, the Gothic hideously misused. The catalogue of horrors went on: Union infantrymen fabricated in zinc, wildly stenciled church interiors, Baroque hatstands, hardly a true muralist or sculptor in sight, nor any fine craftsmanship, no sense of texture, color, scale, proportion; the architect himself, a job-trained businessman, lacking formal education, European travel, a truly national professional organization to defend and discipline him and to put him in touch with his confreres,[5] no journals, no exhibitions, not even any photographs to show him the true look of what he was presumably trying to imitate.[6]

And the Awakening: the Aesthetic Period

In 1870, though, help was on the way. The so-called Aesthetic Movement had begun in England in the early 1860s, and its influence, in the next decade, was to change American architecture, particularly the architecture of the home, dramatically. We have discovered the good qualities of mid-Victorian architecture in the last few years and are disposed to defend it, harshness and all, but it does seem as if cultivated Americans by the early seventies had become bored, ready for something new. Certainly, when Eastlake's *Hints on Household Taste,* published in England in 1868, appeared in the United States in 1872 it was an instant success.[7] Charles Locke Eastlake was a designer annoyed with sculpturesque mid-Victorian furniture, bad workmanship, and kitsch generally, and in his book he explored every art used in furnishing a house, showing original designs and good antiques as indications of what could be done. Included were many of his own designs for furniture, in which the revealed mechanical assemblage of the wooden members and their simple, workmanlike shaping, plus a little carving, formed the whole artistic treatment. The *Gothic Forms* of Bruce Talbert, an even more accomplished Britisher, appeared in America the next year; Eastlake had concentrated on details, but Talbert showed whole interiors, decorated and furnished in a way that combined Eastlakean solidity and rationalism with the mock architectonics of the Victorian Gothicists—gables, arches, columns in miniature.[8] Out of the two sources arose an American "Eastlake," the exaggerated, almost Modernistic, angularity of which annoyed its supposed founder at least as much as the conceits of mid-Victorian England had done. This Eastlake, though, was in the right hands a style of sweet simplicity, and as such deserves more respect than it received in later decades (Fig. 8).

Eastlake and Talbert were part of a greater "Domestic Revival" in England, represented conspicuously by the so-called Queen Anne.[9] In this style, which was evolving rapidly in the early seventies under the influence of Richard Norman Shaw and others, there might indeed be English motifs from the period 1702–14, but so might there be ornament from any reign from Henry VIII through George III. To be Gothic, to be classical, to be authentic at all was not the point; rather, it was to create something comfortable and charming, using anything and everything that served the purpose. So many variations were possible that, since we are treating the subject only in passing, a cliché will have to represent the style as a whole. Imagine, then, a house built of red brick, with ornamental detail in red terra cotta. The basic style is that of the seventeenth-century English country builder, with little pilasters, tall, small-paned windows under segmental arches, and great curvilinear, Dutch-inspired gables. Into the walls are set carved brick or terra-cotta panels showing sunflowers in pots, suggesting typographical ornaments of around 1700. Above the walls rise great hipped roofs, and out of these many tall, ribbed chimneys (Fig. 9). Inside are Georgian, but not too Georgian, mantelpieces, Jacobean paneling, Morris wallpaper, and shelves, many shelves, laden with the collector's items of the period—blue and white ginger jars, majolica jugs, Japanese carvings, fans, vases of peacock feathers. The colors are richly mixed, and the whole quality is relaxed, hedonistic, planned for a life of intelligent, temperate enjoyment of beautiful and curious things (Fig. 10).

The decorative artists of the Aesthetic Movement, producing furniture, textiles, glass, ceramics, and wallpapers, looked to classical antiquity, the Middle Ages, and the eighteenth century for inspiration but also, and increasingly, to Japan.[10] The flat and colorful Japanese print, the *mon* or heraldic badge, the variations on the rectangle of the shoji and on the right angle of the tokonoma, all found their way into the decorative arts.

A few Americans had been aware of these developments before the Centennial, but the British displays at the fair were, to most artists and the public generally, a complete and marvelous surprise. The hospitable St. George's House, the British commissioners' headquarters, was an accomplished work in the Shavian Manorial style, Shaw's half-timbered variant of Queen Anne that, purged of a certain Victorian sharpness, was to have a sixty-year run in the United States (Fig. 11).[11] The best English designers were well represented, and the Japanese, cosmopolites under compulsion since 1854, erected two much admired buildings in their traditional manner; one of these was a bazaar, where American artists eagerly bought up the objects for sale.

Around this time, a native style was being resurrected. In the Romantic period, Colonial architecture had had only a few friends, and was generally regarded as stiff and crude. But the Revolution had its own high romance, and the setting, toward 1876, began to draw luster from the events. A good many Americans summered near old New England towns, and the contrast of these sleepy, old-fashioned places with the city in winter, with its hectic yet formal life, must have helped promote Colonial as the style of a happier period. A "Colonial Revival" began, first as an addition to the Queen Anne vocabulary, then as a distinct style, and later, under Eclecticism, as something stiffer, more symmetrical, more correct, that may be called Neo-Georgian (Fig. 12).[12]

Thus, a rich mixture of motifs became available in the late seventies, which saw the creation of some of the most pleasant domestic architecture ever produced in this country.[13] At first, the sharp forms and hard surfaces of mid-Victorian design remained, but toward 1880 a growing love of texture and plasticity crept in. Brickwork was laid up with raked mortar joints dyed black, and fieldstone, once a cheap, expedient material, became a highly regarded contribution to a growing pallette. The humble wood shingle, which

Americans attempting Shavian Manorial had revived as a siding in place of the strictly British tile-hanging used by Shaw, now began to cover whole walls; stained, creosoted brown, or left to weather silver-gray in sea air, warping and checking, it gave sparkle and subtle color to the walls of houses which, more and more, were leaving off applied decoration. A "Shingle Style" came into being that persisted, in one form or another, for several decades.[14] Out of irreverent borrowings from the English and American past, unpedantic allusions to Japan, and elements of our old vernacular building, we created for a little while something splendidly our own, something that even English, German, and Scandinavian architects soon studied with respect (Figs. 13–15).[15]

Ideas and Education

Meanwhile, various new sources of communication and education were appearing. In the early 1870s New York and Boston architects began to publish "sketch books," in which line and wash drawings, and actual photographs, were reproduced photographically—an expensive process, then and for some time to come.[16] In 1876 our first successful architectural magazine, the *American Architect and Building News,* began publication, and the profession's latent idealism and eagerness for progress at last had a first-class resource.[17] *American Architect* published drawings, and occasionally photographs; it gave practical advice and information; and very importantly, it offered ideas and gave its readers a place to share their own ideas. Other architectural magazines came in the next few years.

In 1870, M.I.T. and the University of Illinois had the only architectural schools in the country, both recently founded; in the next ten years, several others, looking toward Europe for a model, were initiated, and in 1881 the important school at Columbia was established.[18] Before 1870, few students had gone to Paris, to the École des Beaux-Arts, but the Beaux-Arts now became popular. American students abroad naturally went traveling and sketching in various parts of Europe, and saw the true form, scale, color and texture of European architecture at last. In 1883 the first traveling fellowship, the Rotch, was created, and others, including one sponsored by the *American Architect,* followed (Fig. 16).

The client was receiving an education of sorts too. Art magazines and popular periodicals began to discuss the new architecture and decoration, especially in the home, and in the late seventies books concerned both with modern and historic decorative styles began to appear. The old-fashioned Victorian pattern book, supplying designs and plans for builders and their clients, took up the new mode.[19] Aestheticism became fashionable, and of course was overdone. The colors of the interior became too dark and rich, the textures too obtrusive, the accumulation of curious (and possibly beautiful) possessions too great. The standard image of the Victorian interior as a murky obstacle course is less true, surprisingly, of the mid-Victorian living rooms, which tended to be high-ceilinged, airy, and rather sparingly furnished, than of the fashionable city parlor of the mid-eighties. Some decorative artists—for instance Louis Comfort Tiffany, the painter John LaFarge, and the architect Stanford White—did fine interior work around 1880, but too often a historic decorative style, chosen from a book, was adapted, then swamped with fashionable oddments and turned into a kind of bandit's cave (Fig. 17).[20]

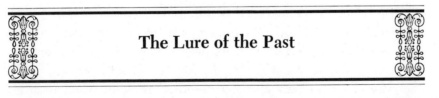

The Lure of the Past

The flood of words and images which had stimulated the Aesthetic movement in America eventually killed it. The Shingle Style, close to being something completely new, was slowly abandoned as architects began to look to eighteenth-century America and the millennia of European history for inspiration even for house architecture. Today, we condemn this: we are annoyed at what seems to be a betrayal of historic truth. We see sentimentalism, supineness, a pandering to the preposterous aspirations of the newly rich. Why, instead of being an Eclectic, was not the young man in architecture around 1890 (a) original and (b) true, in some way to the reality of his own contemporaneous America?

The following is only a guess. The young man in question knew city centers of crowded, dirty, noisy streets, lined with grim buildings in red brick and brownstone, their detailing so many petty illiteracies. The villages were random accumulations of stiff wooden houses, probably in need of paint, enclosed by paling fences, probably out of repair. The factories were hulking brick boxes, surrounded by weeds and trash, that disgorged tired, pale-faced crowds in the evening. These constituted an America of 1890 that seemed to call, not for expression, but for change or decent oblivion. The Shingle Style, admirable for the spreading mass of a large suburban or seaside house, was useless for such architectures of perforated boxes. The problem, rather, was to decorate the perforations and cap the box itself becomingly, and historic architecture had a thousand competent ways of doing both. Furthermore, the young architect's eyes, should he travel, would be opened to marvelous shapes, colors, and textures, most of them reproducible under modern American conditions. Is it surprising that, sketching a Gothic turret in Normandy on some bright morning, recording bit by bit its fine detailing and the accidents of texture left by four hundred years, he might be tempted to re-create the turret, whole and fresh, in Chicago? The careful recording of its lines and surfaces, if his vocation was a true one, was an act of love; its second realization, course by course, in Indiana limestone in the Middle West was perhaps even more so. The mansion, the commercial building, whatever one was designing, would be American enough in its size and proportions, adapted to a program characteristic of its place and time. But, rather than plucking a new style out of the air, why not look to periods, unlike the painful recent past and the unsettled present, when masterly architecture was produced as a matter of course? This is perhaps how the Eclectic around 1890 felt (Fig. 18).

At this point, it is time to introduce a few of the early Eclectics.

Richardson

Henry Hobson Richardson (1838–86) was an individualist, not to be confined to a style or ism, but he managed both to be in the forefront of the Aesthetic movement in America and to create its first Eclectic work—both in collaboration with his gifted draftsman Stanford White.[21] The Watts Sherman house in 1874 at Newport was probably our first realized example of Shavian Manorial— incidentally, it already used shingles as an ersatz for tile-hanging.[22] As to the first Eclectic work, there had been two earlier buildings, both in Boston, that might well have qualified as Eclectic had they not been such isolated performances. The Deacon house of 1847 had a room imitating an eighteenth-century French salon, and another room that incorporated authentic Louis XVI paneling[23]; and the Arlington Street Church of 1859, though executed in brownstone, had a fairly correct Gibbsian design.[24] But Trinity Church in Boston, begun in 1873, seems a more likely candidate (Fig. 19). The style was a development of the Romanesque that Richardson had been using for several years, most conspicuously and successfully at the Brattle Square Church a few blocks away; there, though, the finely colored stonework had been smoothed to a hard surface; here, it was a rugged, "rock-faced" random ashlar, a material then associated with engineering masonry rather than architecture.[25] Inlaid patterns and bands enlivened the surfaces still further, and the apse, whose banding was especially colorful, was imitated from examples, in the Auvergne. The program called for sculpture and painting (this union of the arts, almost unprecedented in America, was to be typical of grand Eclectic projects in later years). It was to be a "color church" inside; the structure was wholly concealed under plasterwork and boarding, which the painter John LaFarge and others covered with a rich green, gold, terra-cotta and blue decoration in which Gothic, Renaissance, and Japanese motifs mingled in a typically Aesthetic manner.[26] Outside, there were to be figures in high relief—these were never carved. But the truly Eclectic feature was the crossing tower. Richardson's original design had called for a two-story structure, the lower story directly over the crossing arches and a badly scaled upper story riding un-

easily inside—a miserable scheme he was wedded to until the building committee, worried about stability, forced him to change it in
about 1874. LaFarge was in Spain around this time, and sent
Richardson a photograph of a crossing tower in Salamanca that
suggested a new solution, one in which the walls would rise sheer
and be capped with a great octagonal pyramid. Richardson sketched
this, White worked it up, and the result was the extremely handsome
design that was executed.[27] The reference to an accurately recorded
"precedent" was typically Eclectic, but so was the smoothing, re-
fining, going-it-one-better, that Richardson and White put into their
adaptation. An expert might recognize the source of the new tower,
but there was really not much resemblance.

Richardson's career has been traced elsewhere; it was a career
that wavered between vigorous originality—among other things he
did excellent Shingle Style work—and reliance on Romanesque and
Byzantine motifs. Both modernists and Eclectics have tried to claim
him as a pioneer, though he was perhaps not a wholly satisfactory
one to either. The modernists see the vigorous man of affairs, the
mighty user of the arch, the man who wanted to design a grain
elevator and the interior of a large river steamboat.[28] The Eclectics
saw the lover of fine materials, the trainer of craftsmen, the man
who would advise a bogged-down designer to "spend an hour with
the photographs." Richardson died of Bright's disease at forty-eight,
and no one can tell what twenty or thirty years more might have
brought, but it is at least possible that if he had had to declare
himself Eclectic or modernist he would have turned more and more
to the photographs. He loved effects; he had a penchant for towers
that were beautiful but more or less useless; he laboriously trans-
ported rugged New England granite to Pittsburgh to face walls of
brick; he loved ornament but was content that it be medieval or
Queen Anne (Figs. 20, 21).[29] He was not an intellectual; when he
wrote, it was factual accounts of his work or the relaxed, rather
facetious letters fashionable in artistic circles in the eighties, not
speculative essays.[30] As Wright noted, he was feeling his way, and it
is possible that out of Romanesque he might have evolved, for better
or worse, as a Gothicist by 1915, the time his career would normally
have ended.

Richardson Romanesque had a great and sudden vogue in the
late eighties and early nineties, especially in Boston, Chicago, and
Pittsburgh, cities where works by the master himself were on view.

Trinity was "low" Episcopal, an auditorium rather than a ritual space, and its broad interior, under a great lantern, was rapidly evolved by Richardson imitators into the "tower" church, whose oversized lantern covered concentric semicircles of pews, while the apse, transepts, and nave became merely vestigial. Richardson's commercial architecture, conceived in great arcades with smaller-scaled fenestration of some sort for the upper stories, was another godsend to the architect who had been trying to tame increasingly tall buildings with Queen Anne or vaguely classical schemes, or was hurling miscellaneous architectural motifs at his façade in the desperate hope of subduing it.[31] Richardson's Romanesque city houses were also imitated widely, and around 1890 a draftsman who could design Byzantine ornament by the yard or the hour must have been a happy and prosperous man.[32] But Richardson was not an easy man to follow. Imitations usually came out meager and disjointed, and perhaps only Harvey Ellis (1852–1904), America's greatest ghost architect and one of our greatest draftsmen, really succeeded in equaling him.[33]

Hunt

Neither Trinity Church nor any other Richardsonian work showed anything like the literalism of imitation that Richard Morris Hunt (1828–95) suddenly introduced, in 1879, in his W. K. Vanderbilt house on Fifth Avenue in New York.[34] Before this Hunt had been, from the Eclectic point of view, of middling interest. He had been the first American to study architecture at the École des Beaux-Arts; had worked under his teacher Lefuel on additions to the Louvre, and then with Thomas Ustick Walter in 1856 on additions to the Washington Capitol. He had won an important lawsuit that helped to establish recognition of the architect as a professional; designed, in 1857, the first studio building in the country, the Tenth Street Studio in New York, where he gave some of the first formal instruction in America in the principles of architecture; and, in 1873, he had designed the Lenox Library in New York, a work later regarded as not too bad. These were minor distinctions, but most of his work thus far had been of the rawest mid-Victorian sort. Now, in the Vanderbilt house, in a period when most of the rich were content to live in boxy, remotely Italianate row houses, and "brownstone" as an adjective equaled "posh," Hunt created a miniature Loire chateau, with correct Louis XII-François I detailing and tall Gothic roofs, executed in pale limestone, a bland, neutral material that was to become very popular for street architecture (Fig. 22).[35] Hunt continued as an architect of chateaus for persons of great wealth, on and off the Avenue. "The Breakers," "Marble House," "Ochre Court," "Belcourt" at Newport, and "Biltmore" near Asheville, show him working on a grand scale for a rising American nobility (Fig. 23). At the same time, he executed a few public commissions: the pedestal of the Statue of Liberty is his, and so is the main entrance of the Metropolitan Museum (Fig. 43).

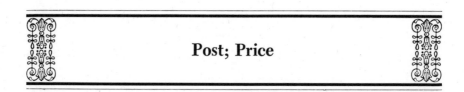

Post; Price

Hunt's work had a certain heaviness, not unpleasant in itself, that was shared by two other architects who should be mentioned briefly, George Browne Post (1837–1913) and Bruce Price (1845–1903).[36] Post had been a draftsman and pupil of Hunt at the Tenth Street Studio, from where he went into independent practice. Mainly a designer of tall commercial buildings, he worked for some years in a magnified Second Empire style, then did a small amount of Queen Anne work and quite a bit of Richardson Romanesque. But for lower and more monumental buildings he had from the first favored a rather sad, arcuated classical manner, sometimes executed in red brick and red terra-cotta as in the New York Produce Exchange and the Long Island Historical Society of the early eighties, but increasingly in beige or ochre brick and terra cotta. This he developed into a tall building style, often with a rather plainly treated shaft concluded by a colonnade of one or more stories. The temple-of-finance formula, passed on from the Greek Revival, was a favorite of his as well, and he used it with grandeur in numerous banks, as well as for the New York Stock Exchange (Fig. 56). Toward the end of his career, Post applied neoclassicism also to his design for the Wisconsin state capitol (Fig. 24). Price is best known today as the architect of a number of important Shingle Style buildings, especially houses at Tuxedo Park, and the first part of the Chateau Frontenac in Quebec. He executed a number of romantically medieval party-wall houses in New York, but developed a classical manner for the city as well; examples are his American Surety Building of 1895 at 100 Broadway (Fig. 25) and his Central Park memorial to Hunt, which he executed with Daniel Chester French.

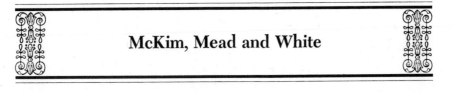

McKim, Mead and White

Two men from Richardson's office, Charles Follen McKim (1847–1909) and Stanford White (1853–1906) were the star performers of the period. [37] In 1872 McKim had inaugurated the Colonial Revival at Newport with pastiche remodeling of a parlor (the mantelpiece was supported by columns copied, apparently, from Early Federal bedposts, and the other detailing was equally loose).[38] Although he tried his hand at Shavian Manorial, he was happiest from the start with the classical styles in their most linear and static forms (Figs. 26, 27). He could create a sumptuous interior, as he did in the Morgan Library, and was quite at home with the grand scale, as Pennsylvania Station showed, but his architecture was basically unsensational, intended for quiet, long-term experience (Figs. 28, 29). It was something to live with; if you liked it at all, you would probably never tire of it. White was a contrasting personality, a painter manqué with a love of brilliant, gorgeous effects.[39] As with Richardson, contemporaries remembered the man as much as the architecture. McKim's background was Philadelphia Quaker, and it showed in his manner. White, on the contrary, had a Rooseveltian dynamism. McKim, with a client, had a persuasive charm (his partners called him Blarney), but White was more inclined to bully his way to the extra ten thousand dollars that made all the difference. He had magpie appetites like those of the Aesthetic period, though with more discrimination; he loved old furniture, old woodwork, old velvets, old ceramics. Under Richardson he had executed Shavian Manorial with great success, and out of this developed free styles even finer. His Newport Casino of 1879 is one of the best Shingle Style buildings; despite a forced picturesqueness, his Tiffany house is a striking work; and two Newport interiors of the same period show him as an original designer of real brilliance (Figs. 30–31).[40] But he took, if you wish, the easy way out and leaned more and more on the historical models favored by Eclecticism (Fig. 32).

McKim, William Rutherford Mead (a "practical man" rather than a designer—his partners called him Dummy), and White formed their partnership in 1879. In the mid-eighties there worked in the office a curmudgeonly draftsman, Joseph Morrill Wells (1853–89), who refused a partnership but who influenced the work of the office greatly.[41] One of several Eclectics of promise who died too soon, Wells loved Quattrocento in its purest Roman form, and when an important commission, the Villard house complex in New York, was turned over to him he adapted a Bramantesque palace in Rome for its façades (Fig. 33). White, who had attempted a design in Romanesque for Villard, caught the spirit of the style and, with help from LaFarge and Saint-Gaudens, he created a series of more or less Quattrocento interiors for Villard's personal residence, rich in marble, mosaic, sculpture, and fine joinery. For ten years afterward, White worked often in Quattrocento. He turned, however, to northern Italy, where early Renaissance was lushly ornate: Madison Square Garden, the Century Club, the Herald building, and numerous other works of around 1890 show his cheerful brick and terracotta variations on the northern Italian theme (Figs 34–37).[42]

These plus a few others, including those venturesome Midwesterners Louis Sullivan and John Wellborn Root, were the architects of greatest stature in 1890. The increasing sophistication that came from the new architectural schools, and from the *American Architect* and other periodicals that the offices were subscribing to, together with the traveling fellowships, began to promote a restless dabbling in various styles like that which had occurred, with much less hard information, around 1850 (Fig. 38). The single-pane plate-glass double-hung window usually remained in 1890, obdurately American of its time, but on the walls around it Heritage swirled fitfully. Romanesque sometimes mixed with French Renaissance, and Quattrocento relaxed its purity. Compositional formulas were stretched in various ways, or multiplied in layers or ranks to fill up commercial fronts of unparalleled dimensions. Sometimes there were too many palmettes, sometimes too much variegated marble, some-times too many motifs that had not been properly integrated with one another, but it was in the main a cheerful confusion (Fig. 39). The 1890 period must have been an absorbing one for the enthusias-tic, the anxious, and the cynical architect alike, for so much was about to happen, could be made to happen.

By the early 1890s, Eclecticism was well established; it was still rather awkward, even in the work of the offices that were setting the new fashions. But, in the eastern United States at least, there was nothing to oppose it.

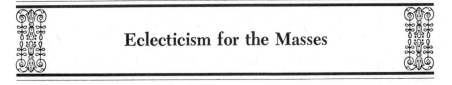

Eclecticism for the Masses

Until the 1880s, the urban middle-class homemaker had been limited to conventional red brick and clapboard and to the conven-tional sash window, about three feet wide. Doorframes and window caps were optionals that varied in design more or less as the prevail-ing high-style architecture did, but the pedestrian of 1880, taking a sight toward the end of a residential street, usually saw a double row of house fronts without glaring incongruities. Main Street, how-ever, was commercial, and a druggist, a dentist, and a lawyer might share a palazzo of thirty front feet with a very different sort of palazzo next door. Toward 1890, though, Main Street standards were brought to the residential street. Roman brick, rock-faced ashlar, terra-cotta, pressed tin, and other materials were now available, and so were miniature turrets, fake roofs, fake gables, authentic finials, and a host of other novelties. A chateau with party walls is a chateau nonetheless if you want to see it that way, and many apparently did. In Philadelphia, a "city of homes" according to an old bromide, semidetached houses—Roman brick and sheet metal on the front and common brick elsewhere—were built in sprawling uniform masses from 1890 to 1920; and their successors, vulgar-genteel rows with sheet-metal shutters, fake roofs, and Colonial doorways of cement, are still going up in the area. Philip Wylie described the common man as the hero's backside, and this sort of speculative and vernacular building was the backside of the true Eclectic, who demanded a fine palette of materials that he knew how to handle; but all too many others engaged in the act of building did not.

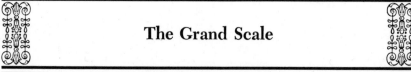

The Grand Scale

In 1893, the Eclectics had a show of power—not a uniformly brilliant demonstration, but certainly one that opened the eyes of the country. This was the World's Columbian Exposition, inaugurated a year late to celebrate the four hundredth anniversary of the discovery of America.[43] Burnham and Root of Chicago had been made the artistic directors of the fair, and Olmsted, taking a swampy patch of public land on the outskirts of the city, developed it as a romantic park, with a formal Court of Honor at the center (Fig. 40).[44] Root, who in his tentative way was looking ahead to a new American architecture, began sketches for major buildings, but died. Daniel Hudson Burnham (1846–1912), his partner, called in architects, many from the East, to supply the buildings.[45] Eclectic classicists predominated (Fig. 41). A general agreement was swiftly reached that the architecture around the Court of Honor should all be classical and that the main cornice level should be sixty feet— quite a tall order. Somebody, whose identity was later forgotten, said, "Let's paint it all white!" It was done, and Americans were staggered. Most of them had never seen anything remotely like it. Not only were the giant orders, executed in staff (i.e., fibrous plaster), a brisker summing-up of a tall façade than they were used to, but the comprehensiveness of the design, the experience of great vistas framed by harmonious buildings, was new.

Not only the architects were on display. Their friends in the figurative arts, which had been having their own renaissance, enriched the fair with paintings and sculptures. All the arts were represented at the policy meetings. As the decisions and proposals came, a commissioner of the fair, moved by the grand vision appearing, blurted out, "Oh gentlemen, it is a dream"—not condescendingly, but as one who hoped, against hope, to see it realized. And Saint-Gaudens came over to Burnham, during a lull in the discussions, and exclaimed, "Look here, old fellow, do you realize that this is the greatest meeting of artists since the fifteenth century?"

The White City, as the fair was often called, was a major early monument of a decade when whiteness seemed to have suddenly invaded architecture, recently red and brown (Fig. 42). One may point to white terra-cotta, white marble and granite, white limestone, white paintwork—to exteriors and interiors all white or white in connection with the golden brown of Roman brick, the pale yellow or gray of Colonial Revival clapboards, variegated marble, gilding. There was also, now, the Great White Way of the big city, thanks to electricity. Even the Navy, of late, had white-hulled warships with gilded scrollwork at the bows and buff superstructures.

The giant scale had appeared even before 1893. Mid-Victorian architecture had had tall interiors, but it emphasized the individual story in the façade. By 1890 the façade, except in that abnormality the skyscraper, was treated more and more as a single grand gesture from bottom to top. A portico was not a porch but an honorific device; uselessly broad and shallow, it rose two or three stories to help its building, which might otherwise be just a big, windowed box, to cut a figure in the world (Fig. 43). The very rich had their own gigantism, variously expressed in towers, pavilions, and loggias, in marble, mosaics, ponderous antiques, and tapestries. Shingle Style houses ceased to be adequate as summer places for such persons, though the merely well-to-do still built these and Colonial Revival houses. Great wealth was pretentious and ambitious, and spent money on showy architecture (Fig. 44). (Later, the miniature Blois or Versailles, though it did not wholly disappear, yielded pride of place to an updated Shavian Manorial, an artful combination of quaint, even pseudo-humble, elements strung out to the length of the client's purse, or to classicism of a homier sort.)

The Beaux-Arts Style

In the mid-nineties a brash and energetic style, the Beaux-Arts, came to the American city (Fig. 45).[46] The École des Beaux-Arts had been the model for the evolving American architectural school, and it had become fashionable to study there, at least for a final polish, if one could. Its curriculum was primarily for the French student, however. Shaped by Colbert's policy, under Louis XIV, of making French art a standardized high-quality product at the service of the state, it combined ideals of beauty and clear planning with a certain civil-service pragmatism. Its student problems varied from a demand to whip up a sketch design for a minor construction in a few hours, to a competition, whose detailed program was announced months in advance, for the Prix de Rome, which gave the winner, a French national always, four years at the Villa Medici and guaranteed government employment on his return.

White's essays in Italian Renaissance and McKim's quieter classicism, taken up intelligently and unintelligently by many others, were in the long run to be the styles of the center city, but there were many for whom they were at once too quiet and too demanding. And to these the Beaux-Arts style, almost a mid-Victorian revival, seemed just the right thing. Back came the mansard roofs, the rustication, the columns and entablatures standing boldly forth from the wall, of the most sumptuous Victorian Second Empire.[47] But while that had been a rather lean style, slightly impatient somehow, the Beaux-Arts favored the big, broad gesture. Reaching back into French architecture as far back as François I, it assembled motifs in a way which, if they never violated axial symmetry, had almost a Queen Anne looseness. The slightly overdone was the essence of its very real charm. Ionic columns were a little too thick, even chubby, and from their correct Roman volutes depended unnecessary strings of husks. The mansard roof swelled, and an elaborate cheneau at its curb created as fancy a skyline as the cast-iron *passementeries* of the mid-Victorian counterpart. Frivolous young ladies, eight feet high, stood on ledges, holding wreaths or blowing post-horns. French windows, with sinuous tracery that may have been a discreet nod to Art Nouveau, opened onto balconies supported by massive, heavily sculptured consoles. Ernest Flagg, the most skillful user of the style, and a few others refined it now and again into something truly urbane, playing off overscaled voids and underscaled ornament, much of it in wrought iron, in such a way that they balanced handsomely (Fig. 46).[48]

Beaux-Arts was used especially in New York and perhaps no style has been more sympathetic, in several senses, to such a vast and hustling city. The skyscrapers of the 1920s are handsome but self-centered, and the later ones are mere business suits; but the innumerable hotels, apartment houses, town mansions, loft buildings, and theaters in Beaux-Arts seem warm by contrast. Slightly silly, big as they are, offering their tawdry proliferation of heavy ornamental trinkets for admiration, they mingle an endearing jollity with their grandeur (Figs. 47–54).

 ## "The Scale Is Roman, and It Will Have to Be Sustained" (McKim)

The big city, however, was destined for a more correct, more rectilinear, classicism. "Fine" streets, like Euclid Avenue in Cleveland, had existed in mid-Victorian times, but without any special precautions to keep them fine. The center of town was usually an incoherent agglomeration of tall buildings and low ones, wagons, cable cars, and pedestrians—romantic or messy, depending on whether you were O. Henry or Henry James. But the White City suggested that the town square and the park, already set apart as places of beauty, might be extended in the form of grand avenues through the center of the city. The ideal of the "City Beautiful," nebulously in existence even before 1893, took form.[49] Washington, planned as a City Beautiful from the start, had been mishandled in the Victorian years—there was, for example, a railroad station on the Mall—and the rehabilitation and extension of the L'Enfant plan was an obvious desideratum. Burnham, in collaboration with Mc-Kim and other architects, drew up plans for landscaping, the relocation of existing facilities, and the siting of future monuments.[50] Burnham went on to draw up plans for the centers of San Francisco and Cleveland, and the Philippine cities of Manila and Baguio, and in 1909 produced a plan for Chicago that was in part realized.[51] Other cities attempted, or thought about, similar measures. In Philadelphia, a few citizens pushed through the Benjamin Franklin Parkway, slicing across Thomas Holme's seventeenth-century gridiron to move automobile traffic to the western and northern suburbs and to form a Parisian setting for the public institutions of the city. An art museum on a grand terrace, a reef before which many cars have been wrecked, terminated the Parkway's axis at one end; the other was terminated by City Hall, the ultimate Second Empire building in America. In between were to have been, among other things, two cathedrals. (This nineteenth-century quarter of the city, especially the wedge between the Parkway and the Schuylkill river, has never recovered from a foreign-body reaction.)[52]

Individual buildings followed the grand design too. Specific precedents were useful at times for these, but usually a solid grounding in the Five Orders and the standard devices tested and accepted by classicists throughout history gave enough inspiration in the first twenty years of this century. Immigration from Italy provided stoneworkers, mosaicists, terra-cotta workers, and craftsmen of other kinds at not excessive wages to execute the fine detail of the new buildings (Figs. 55–62). A boon to architects who wanted great interior spaces was the system of Rafael Guastavino, a Catalan engineer who modernized traditional tile vaulting—the Catalans were wizards at vaulting even in the Middle Ages—for use in modern construction. Many of the Roman domes, Gothic vaults, and geometrical staircases of the Eclectic period were built by R. Guastavino and Co. as shell constructions of thin tile and strong mortar.[53] The tall office building was now steel-framed as a matter of course, and the diminution of wall thickness from bottom to top was a thing of the past. Somewhat in the spirit of Sullivan's recommendations in the 1890s, the first story or two, devoted to shops and special spaces, were treated as a base; the common rental spaces above, as a rather plain shaft; and the upper few stories as an ornate capital, terminated by a great cornice.[54] Most Eclectics expressed this formula by putting a fantastically heightened palazzo on top of a temple. Later, such a solution, as we shall see, ceased to be viable, but for the time being it was standard.

 ## The Eclectic and the Engineer

The raw bones of the skyscraper could be hidden—had to be, indeed, because it was early discovered that fire could bend, if not burn, the structural metal. Not all metallic structures hid behind terra cotta, though, and the Eclectic was uneasy when faced with its primitive forms (Fig. 63). A ship, on the face of it, was as *sachlich* a construction as you could find. (Actually, naval architects "styled" passenger vessels; big ocean liners, and even river boats, might have dummy funnels, and yachts had exaggeratedly raking sterns.) But the ship's interior designer favored motifs imitating land architecture. A ship of 1910 in a heavy sea, its openings firmly shut against towering waves and without stabilizers to ease the rolling, was a miserable place to be, and the decor of a country-house parlor reminded the passenger of happier things (Figs. 64–65).[55]

Civil engineering, very conspicuous and unconcealed, was another problem. One naturally envisions an engineering work as a geometrical form, perhaps a bridge ideally proportioned to its load and so lithe, so simple, that not even the most self-serving architect would want to tamper with it. Unfortunately, this was not always so. The curve of a great steel arch or the catenary of a suspension bridge might indeed read as a classical line of beauty, to which adventitious adornment would be as dime-store rings on Paderewski's hand, but what of the massive anchorage of the suspension bridge, the abutment of the arch, or worse yet, the amorphous railroad bridge, meant to function as a beam or a cantilever depending on where the train was (Fig. 66)?

An engineering work did not usually follow an ideal shape; but was rather an assemblage of standard rolled steel sections, cut to length and assembled in an expedient manner, and joined to the earth by something of the earth, either masonry or concrete—a vague mass that called out for "treatment." When the work was conspicuous a gracious gesture was expected, and architect and engineer alike floundered in making it.[56] Sometimes they hoped that pinnacles would do the trick, or steel brackets shaped with a certain Beaux-Arts verve, or a casing in ashlar.[57] We can sympathize; on the one hand, the Eclectics were surely too narrow in their conceptions of beauty and went too far in the matter of treatment, but on the other hand the structure itself was often ugly because its realized form was not obviously meaningful. Today we have not really solved the problem. Conditions in Switzerland at the time Maillart worked allowed him to shape reinforced concrete into a bone for spanning a gorge, and to create a beautiful bridge. In modern America, we use economical steel beams on concrete bents spaced at expedient intervals, and it is obvious that beauty does not really matter; no scored rustication on the concrete can disguise the fact.

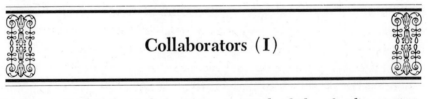

Collaborators (I)

The architect depended of course on the help of other artists, and on a host of craftsmen and suppliers who could meet or anticipate his wishes. The major Eclectic building called for a union of the arts; above the cornice of the great hall was a vault to be frescoed, and sculpture outside was needed to recall historic worthies, or humanize—up to a point—abstract virtues. And the building, unless it was right at the sidewalk's edge, had to have its proper entourage of trees, shrubs, steps, and paths.

LaFarge, as we have seen, led the way for the painters in the mid-seventies. In 1879 William Morris Hunt, brother of Richard

Morris Hunt, made another valiant try at monumental art in the Assembly Chamber at the Albany capitol, just completed by the Victorian Gothicist Leopold Eidlitz. But no work of art, decor on the *Titanic* apart, has been more utterly doomed from the start. Hunt was offered two cramped lunettes over ranges of windows, whose light by day interfered with the view of his compositions, the *Discoverer* and *The Flight of Night*; furthermore, Eidlitz's vaulting had bold pseudo-medieval striping that clashed hideously with Hunt's painterly and low-keyed works. Worse yet, out of ignorance, Hunt had painted on plaster improperly laid on the walls, which were too damp to hold the paint. As the final blow, settling of the building made the vaults dangerous; the acoustics had already proved to be impossible, so the vaults were demolished, and a ceiling installed below the lunettes. Hunt died the next year—possibly in grief over this fiasco—but his paintings were remembered with admiration even after mural programs, carried out with perfect competence, had long been expected in great public works.[58]

A few private decorative commissions had been carried out by the time of the World's Columbian, and the Boston Public Library was planned around 1890 for an ambitious set of frescoes by Puvis de Chavannes, Abbey, and Whistler (his was never executed), as well as a set, part painting, part low-relief sculpture, by Sargent. But it was the fair itself that gave most Americans, even cultured urbanites, their first look at grand interiors painted with the mixture of allegory and decoration that was to become fairly common in the next forty years. To give an account of the major works and the major artists who flourished before 1915 is impossible here; one would have to trace the careers of John LaFarge, Edwin Howland Blashfield (Fig. 67), Kenyon Cox, Elihu Vedder, and many others in the earlier years, taking also into account contributions by Maxfield Parrish, Howard Pyle, and similar smaller-scale painters who turned their hands now and then to monumental work. After 1910 or so, there would be newcomers to reckon with—Barry Faulkner, Frank Brangwyn, and Ezra Winter, for example—and new approaches to color and line. For that matter, one would be tempted to go right on into the work of the Federal Artists' Project of the 1930s, even though the allegorical representations of high Eclecticism were, in that unhappy period, replaced by the life of The People. Even more than Eclectic architecture, Eclectic painting —to risk the name—demands an extension of tolerance these days, a willingness to see whether there may not be quality in it after all. A Howard Pyle ship is a quaint, dumpy seventeenth-century affair, portrayed literally, totally unlike, say, a John Marin yacht; and we may wonder whether Jack Levine, rather than Edwin Howland Blashfield, would not have been the man to sum up the civic attributes of Hudson County, New Jersey. We are skeptical of allegories and Bacchic processions and wonder how a real artist—if the muralist of the 1900s indeed *was* one—could waste his time on such empty-headed stuff. Let us look, though; let us go off to the local courthouse and give the painter, and ourselves, a real chance.

As with the painter, so with the sculptor—except that the sculptor had been working with the architect since Early Federal times.[59] He had not exactly been spoiled with architectural commissions, but a certain number of pediments, niches, and pedestals had been made available to him over the years; for instance, the Philadelphia City Hall, begun in 1874, fairly seethes with the sometimes totally mysterious sculpture of Alexander Milne Calder. Much mid-Victorian sculpture was like a great deal of its architecture, in having perfection of an obvious, technically oriented sort. Whether in marble or in bronze, it suggested that a cast had been taken of the subject without disturbing his hair or his uniform in the process. A mid-Victorian battle group, such as those by Levi Scofield on Public Square in Cleveland, is a frozen moment like that in the photograph of the Iwo Jima flag-raising: the flag, torn by shot and the wind, is almost as thin as cloth, and every tassel on its bullion fringe is going its separate way. During the Eclectic period, this ultranaturalism yielded to more summary effects. As the classical Eclectic building became denser and more unified, so did its sculpture, although of course to varying degrees with different artists. At the World's Columbian there had been, with the sculpture as with the architecture, a tendency for each component to stand apart a little too much from the ensemble—although French's statue of the Republic and Saint-Gaudens' *Diana*, atop the Agriculture Building, suited their settings beautifully. (Ten years later, at the height of Beaux-Arts, a great consumer of sculpture in varied forms—garlands, consoles, cheneaux, figures of solemn allegorical import and half-dressed women whose only function was to cheer things up—the relation of the sculpture to the building was fortunately better understood [Fig. 68].) As a more sober classicism prevailed, the role of sculpture became increasingly restricted: an occasional statue in a niche or on a pedestal, taking up a clearly defined place in the ensemble, and of course the more or less standard capitals, consoles, and string-courses. With the advent of Art Deco around 1925 and the greatly simplified classicism that had a vogue around 1930, there was a call for highly stylized bas-reliefs to cover panels and friezes. Paul Manship had already introduced such simplification, quite gracefully, into freestanding sculpture, and Lee Lawrie, working with Bertram Goodhue on his later designs, had actually used giant allegorical busts to terminate architectural masses, whose planes gradually divided as they rose to become stylized surfaces of flesh and costume. Again, it is possible only to mention a few names: Karl Bitter, who worked with Hunt at Biltmore, Chicago, and elsewhere, and with Post at the Wisconsin state capitol[60]; Augustus Saint-Gaudens, a frequent collaborator with White and McKim, whose *Farragut* and *Sherman* in New York are perhaps the best-known of many works[61]; Daniel Chester French, sculptor of the *Lincoln* in the Lincoln Memorial in Washington[62]; Paul Manship, best known for the Prometheus Fountain at Rockefeller Plaza in New York[63]; Adolph Weinman, who worked with McKim and White on Pennsylvania Station and the Madison Square Presbyterian Church, and whose designs for our silver currency were used for many years.

From the 1880s on, the architect with a large practice was pressured more and more into becoming the president of a company rather than an artist. Minor work had to be turned over to draftsmen entirely—this was true even in Richardson's case—and some architects, once their practices reached a certain size, no longer designed at all, while others took a business partner to leave themselves free. To say that an architect "designed" a certain building often means merely that he approved a design that went out under his name. Burnham, for instance, was a man of ideas, and one who knew how to get them realized, rather than a designer; gifted at conceiving the general plan of a commercial building or a city, he entrusted the actual designs to others, such as Charles B. Atwood (1849–95), whose Peristyle and Fine Arts Building at the World's Columbian were among its most-applauded works and whose Reliance Building for D. H. Burnham and Company is regarded as one of the best early skyscrapers.[64]

Then there were the craftsmen: the assistants of the sculptors and muralists; the decorators, an emerging tribe some of whom were solely designers, some of whom designed and sold ornamentation on special order, and some of whom sold and assembled ready-made stock ornament; the glassmakers, ironmakers, and carvers, who might be either artists or skilled executants; the mosaicists, workers in scagliola, bronzefounders, and many others; and the suppliers of an ever-increasing range of fine materials—brick, terra cotta, marble, ashlar, veneer wood, and so on (Figs. 69, 70).

An Eclectic building of the first order was a fantastically expensive undertaking; it might demand that hundreds of tons of granite be railroaded hundreds of miles, and it certainly required hours of thought and effort from some of the country's most eminent artists. Though the walls cost thousands for every foot they rose, there were oceans of empty space, four-fifths of which were not for light, or ventilation, or headroom, but simply for aesthetic pleasure. Cut-rate and second-rate Eclecticism was thus inevitable: stock ornament, cheaply cast or fabricated in pressed tin; boxy apartment houses with minimal lobbies and slovenly proportions, designed to formula; guides to detailing for the untrained and untalented; face-brick street fronts and common-brick sides and backs. Nor was every architect a sophisticated artist—far from it. Just as they do today, the hacks studied the latest issues of the magazines and reproduced the fashionable effects. If they needed special help, there were tramp draftsmen such as Harvey Ellis who had a feeling for the style of choice and who would stop in long enough to do the general design.[65]

The Second Generation

By the early 1900s some of the first Eclectics were already dead. White was murdered in 1906 by a lunatic; McKim failed in health, then died in 1909. Burnham lasted until 1912. Designers of great promise, Joseph Wells, Charles Atwood, Halsey Wood, had died prematurely, even before 1900. But by 1900, a new generation of Eclectics was already at work. A few of the most famous names will have to suffice here.

Cass Gilbert (1859–1934), a former McKim, Mead and White draftsman, designed the New York Custom House, the Woolworth Building, the U.S. Army Supply Base in Brooklyn, and the U.S. Court House in New York, as well as many buildings in other parts of the country (Fig. 71).[66] Thomas Hastings (1860–1929), after early days with the Herter Brothers, famous decorators, and with McKim, Mead and White, joined another draftsman from the latter office to found Carrere and Hastings, the firm which designed the New York Public Library and the Fifth Avenue mansion of H. C. Frick (Figs. 53, 72).[67]

Arthur Brown, Jr. (1874–1957), of Bakewell and Brown of San Francisco, executed the grandly classical City Hall there and later worked on the Federal Triangle in Washington (Fig. 73).[68] And again in San Francisco, there was Bernard Maybeck (1862–1957), a former Carrere and Hastings draftsman who, as everyone knows, moved blithely in and out of any number of styles.[69] Ernest Flagg (1857–1947) worked in a Beaux-Arts manner that was now robust, now refined, and Henry Hornbostel (1867–1961)[70] designed grandly in the same style for New York bridges and Pittsburgh campuses (Figs. 74, 75).[71] John Russell Pope (1874–1937) specialized, but not exclusively, in classicism.[72] Horace Trumbauer (1869–1938) had one of the largest practices; the works of his office included the Widener Library at Harvard, the Art Museum and the Free Library in Philadelphia (Fig. 76), and a great many mansions in the Louis XV and Louis XVI styles in Newport and New York. A good example of the non-designing architect, Trumbauer left much of this work to a black designer on his staff, Julian Abele. The above constitute, of course, a mere sampling of the architects who were at work in every metropolitan area at this time.

After 1890, cities began to build upward at a great rate and soon office buildings, government buildings, hotels, and other new constructions at the center of even a medium-sized town were inclined to project a metropolitan image: a box of stone or textured red brick, with a flaring cornice above and rustication below executed in stone or white terra cotta, and many, many windows in between.

The educational development of the profession had not stood still. The number of American schools had grown, and a favorite project of McKim's had been realized: an American Academy in Rome where promising students of architecture and the decorative arts, by carefully devolping their proven talents and by the mere fact of being in Italy and using their eyes—observing the art, the streets, the sky, and indeed everything—could be infused with a beauty that would perfect their own art. *American Architect*, still in existence, had by the 1900s been joined by other magazines, most conspicuously *Architectural Record*, which published Montgomery Schuyler's critiques and also gave Frank Lloyd Wright a national rostrum.[73]

The Panama-Pacific Exposition, 1915

In 1915 an exposition was held in San Francisco to celebrate the opening of the Panama Canal.[74] As with the 1893 fair, this provided a showcase for the more exalted forms of contemporary Eclecticism, and particularly large-scale urban classicism. The architectural approach, this time, was somewhat different. Rather than attempting to unify a number of very different buildings, grouped loosely around a court of honor, by a uniform cornice line and a universal whiteness, the artistic directors planned the main exposition buildings (or "palaces") in a closely knit complex, meant from the outside to suggest a walled town: great pedestrian avenues, intersecting in courts, passing from side to side and end to end, with Maybeck's Palace of Fine Arts as the terminal feature of the central avenue (Figs. 77, 78). The outer walls of the complex were symmetrical, but inside the treatment varied as one passed through the avenues and courts. Another innovation was in the use of color. Jules Guerin, a muralist, renderer, and illustrator who had a fine sense of color, was called in to suggest a chromatic treatment suited to the uncertain light of San Francisco. He decided that the "masonry" (actually staff) should be colored and textured in imitation of travertine (even a locomotive, stationed to provide steam for a display, was painted to imitate travertine) and that this prevailing grayish tan should be set off with accents of burnt orange, vivid blue, and other rich colors.

Although much of the art, the sculpture especially, was decidedly mediocre, the Panama-Pacific must have been a beautiful exposition. Most of the crudities and uncertainties of 1893 had been eliminated, and the walk up the central avenue on a fine evening toward the Palace of Fine Arts must have been one of the most delightful experiences American architecture had ever offered.

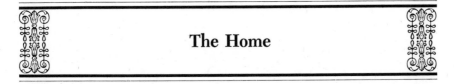

The Home

Though the grand classical architecture of the city occupied the center of the stage in the prewar period, it was not owing to any lack in, or of, domestic architecture in these years.

Out in the suburbs, near the ends of the files of lamp standards and trees on the new boulevards, houses were rising in areas where the formalities of downtown were relaxed, and gables and artfully rounded eaves of Ruberoid (in imitation of thatch) expressed, or overexpressed, the simplicity of life in middle-class America. The Shingle Style had not died, though it was fading away; it had blended with the ascendant Colonial Revival, mainly, or had survived in its pure guise of stained shingles and rough masonry mostly in boxy little houses that totally lacked the placticity of 1880. Shingled houses of 1910 or even 1920 were not uncommon, but the surfaces were usually negative, cut up by windows and doors whose trim had become the positive design element. The texturalism of residential architecture current at this time, which exploited the roughness and variegation possible in brick, stone, slate, and tile to the point of abuse, forgot the corduroy browns or silver-grays of the unpainted shingle, perhaps because it was associated with the tentative, offhand, lowercase eclecticism of the Aesthetic period, now left behind.

The Colonial Revival, begun as another ingredient, a Queen Anne variant, in the Aesthetic mix, had emerged as early as 1879 as a style in its own right (Fig. 79). Shingles yielded to clapboards, painted yellow, gray, or white, and lavish amounts of white trim flowered on these new, neutral surfaces. Symmetry, a withdrawal from the picturesque, became increasingly common. The playful roof of the 1880s was replaced by a standard hipped or gabled one, at first a little too steep, pierced by rows of dormers, and a little too big and flashy. At the center of the façade a doorway, usually elaborate, one that a whale-blubber baron might have commanded a century before, stood between big broad windows in which persisted the Queen Anne compromise of a single sheet of plate glass below and many small panes above—now arranged in a vaguely Georgian tracery pattern. In spite of this reliance on the past the house remained, most definitely, a house of 1890 or 1900. There was often a big porch, precedent to the contrary, and some philistines held onto the corner tower of the 1880s. This Colonial Revival, if it made for a more mannered, more rigid, perhaps less interesting house than the Shingle Style had done, was still concerned with producing a building to be lived in rather than looked at, one whose ample proportions suggested light, air, and space. It is not surprising that funeral directors are among the most conscientious preservers of such houses: not only does the four-square plan, with its big parlors, accommodate the public side of their operation comfortably, but the houses themselves, when well maintained, have a cheerful, solid, reassuring look, an ointment for the sting of death.

After 1900 further refinement set in: the symmetry was perfected, the proportions corrected, the style purified, and the Colonial Revival became just a shade pedantic. Indeed, after 1900 or 1910 it is more fitting to speak of Neo-Georgian, a serious and learned style then becoming increasingly popular for houses, churches, schools, and indeed buildings of almost every sort.[75]

Similar purification was taking place inside the house. The deep colors and random accumulations of the 1880s had been chased away by the end of the next decade, at least in fashionable homes, and it came to seem evident that façades, decorations, and furnishings should conform, as a general rule, to some one historic style. Books on interior decoration were still being published, and more and more showed historic interiors, usually palatial, as models. Edith Wharton wrote an influential work in the nineties with the architect Ogden Codman, and in the furnishing of her own eighteenth-century house in France, the "Pavillon Colombe," drew the reproach that she was *too* correct—that a French family would have been more casual, less pure. A similar rigidity affected some of our stay-at-homes; and yet, even when the potted palms and ferns of 1900 had followed the bric-a-brac into oblivion, many a room had a Morris chair, an opalescent glass lamp, or some recent and mildly "modern" portrait to drive away the faint must of the archaeological.[76]

The rich were becoming less ostentatious. Indeed, in the years after 1900 the mansion began, slowly, to become more informal, more picturesque, even as the Colonial Revival of the middle class began to stiffen (Figs. 80, 81). Chateaus and Trianons, both grand and petty, were still being built, with their large formal gardens, but these frontal attacks on the visitor were beginning to seem a little obvious (Figs. 82, 83). Many persons of wealth preferred what were, essentially, nice big houses, with a little agreeable pomp around the doorways and deep loggias that carried on the tradition of the porch. French windows opened from light, airy halls onto terraces, and stairs with wrought-iron balustrades led upward to long, paneled bedroom corridors. Perhaps the best country-house designer of the post-1900 period was Charles Platt (1861–1933), whose houses borrowed from the Georgian period, the Italian Renaissance, and the French eighteenth century without being heavily in debt to any one of these, and whose gardens—he was a landscape architect too—had an intimate, delicate, Maxfield Parrish charm (Figs. 84, 85).[77]

The literature of homemaking continued; indeed, the homemaker of the 1900s was bombarded with it. For the rich, there were books showing contemporary mansions—for a few years, in fact, there was an annual.[78] To these, around 1910, began to be added the folio monographs on the major Eclectics, particularly the house designers, that would continue until after 1940—well-illustrated books, with photos, sketches, measured drawings, and plans. The "shelter" magazines, now abundant, told the homemaker how to plan and furnish; Gustav Stickley's *Craftsman* gave him the Arts and Crafts viewpoint, but most of the others, published in New York or Boston, kept up with the recent trends in Eclectic architecture, decoration, and furnishing. There were books, as well, on the construction of bungalows, and even of houseboats.[79]

Yet it was not a foregone conclusion, around 1910, that a house should be designed in a historic style. In the Chicago area, and elsewhere in the Middle West, the Prairie School—Frank Lloyd Wright and many others—continued active until around 1915, but even apart from their work there were many, many houses that had little or no relation to any style. In some cases, this was a matter of necessity; the prefabricated Aladdin Homes that came shipped on flatcars (for between $374.30 and $3,959.60 C.O.D. in 1918) were made with too great an economy of means to look like much of anything.[80] The Craftsman home (of which Harvey Ellis was an occasional designer) was simple by choice, and so too were the bungalow, very popular around 1910, and the mountain lodge, where massive logs (or what seemed to be massive logs) were de rigueur inside and out.

Even the major Eclectics, at the heights of their careers, laid the Styles aside when they had a residential commission where informality seemed part of the cultural context. With the Villard complex already built, McKim, Mead and White designed that no longer existent masterpiece of Shingle Style architecture, the Low house at Bristol, R.I., a giant gable with the roof slopes going the "wrong" way; and John Russell Pope was neither Roman nor Tudor, but mostly emphatically rustic, in a summer camp he did in upper New York State.

But there was a large measure of originality even to many comfortable middle-class houses of 1910. Executed in wood, fieldstone, or one of the proliferation of face bricks available by then, these houses, in their massing and ornament, allude to, rather than follow, historic precedent. Sometimes the influence of English suburban architecture, based on the farmhouse vernacular, sets the general tone, sometimes the Colonial, sometimes even the Dutch Colonial, with its gambrel roofs and shed dormers. But sometimes, too, the house is a solid cube, with simplified detailing that seems almost to recall the Greek Revival or Italian Villa styles of sixty or seventy years before (Fig. 86).

The Mild Innovators

Such "modernism," however, was modernism by default, coming about more from an indifference to questions of style than a conscious intention to develop an idiom appropriate to contemporary

America. In the search for new forms, nevertheless, Sullivan, Wright, and the Prairie School architects were not wholly alone. In Pittsburgh, for instance, Frederick Scheibler (1872–1958) produced a number of handsome apartment houses and homes, much influenced by avant-garde Austrian and German architecture of the pre-Gropius period (Fig. 87).[81] In California, Louis Christian Mullgardt (1866–1942) not only designed a number of handsome, highly simplified houses, almost Himalayan in appearance, but contributed to the Panama-Pacific Exposition its most original work, the Court of Ages (or of Abundance), heroically scaled and exotically decorated in a way that owed something, but not too much, to the earliest Spanish Renaissance (Fig. 89).[82]

A much-published advocate of a new style was Claude Bragdon (1866–1946), architect, stage designer, and mystic, friend of Sullivan and translator of Ouspensky.[83] In *Projective Ornament* he began a crusade to make mathematical formulas the basis not only for architectural composition—nothing new, of course,—but also for a system of ornament appropriate to our science-oriented civilization. Until 1942 he put his lucid prose and very fine draftsmanship at the service of his two great interests, a form of theosophy and a new system of ornament based on whirling squares, magic squares, and projections of three- and indeed of four-dimensional figures. His architectural book *The Frozen Fountain* is handsome indeed, for his use of black on white is as fine as Beardsley's, and if the world he illustrates is static, and even a little sacerdotal in feeling (as anything "promoted" in a high-class manner in this period tends to be), it is marvelously elegant and serene, wrapped up in a very pleasant sort of Eternal Now (Fig. 88).

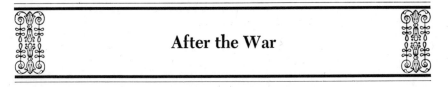

After the War

Around 1915 the great period of classical urban architecture began to come to an end. So many courthouses, post offices, clubhouses, museums, and libraries had been built in the recent past that the need for these was declining. The town mansion had already begun to yield in popularity to the cheaper and more convenient apartment house, whose anonymity had caused it to be rejected by many people up until then. Such apartment houses were almost always classical at first, but soon were built in all styles, traditional and modern. Another alternative was just as popular: the suburb and the country estate, accessible by train or trolley or new and well-made parkways (or for rich shore-dwellers, by special "commuter" yachts).

But commercial architecture was the first to break with the prevailing classicism. The palazzo skyscraper of 1900, a prism of space filled to whatever level the owner wished, had gone too far in New York, and the Zoning Law of 1916, in order to allow a minimal amount of light and air into the streets, imposed a ziggurat-like form, possibly with a central tower, once walls on the property line had reached a certain height. A classical ziggurat (Fig. 90) was possible, to be sure, and some were attempted, but their effect was almost bound to be awkward, and architects began to look for ways to treat the many setbacks necessary to use all the allowable space in a more positive way. At first, as we shall see, medieval styles seemed to offer great promise, with their precedents of masses rising behind masses, pinnacles behind pinnacles, but in the long run it seemed best to find new forms.

The Gothic

The major alternative to a classical style was, of course, a Gothic one, and by 1915 a large amount of very polished Gothic had been executed, mainly for churches and educational institutions.

While the Domestic Revival was revolutionizing the home in the 1870s Gothic continued to be the undisputed style for churches, and found a fair amount of use as well in academic buildings, town halls, commercial buildings, and even, still, in houses. Upjohn and Renwick were still practicing in 1870, though they were nearing the ends of their careers. Upjohn's son Richard M. Upjohn was at work on the Hartford capitol through the seventies. In Boston, in 1871, Sturgis and Brigham began the Museum of Fine Arts—on Copley Square, site of Trinity Church and the library. (Here, by the way, architectural terra cotta, shipped from England, had its first large-scale use in the United States.)[84] The veteran Gothicist Leopold Eidlitz, toward the end of the seventies, began his half of the continuing work on the Albany capitol—the other half was Richardson's —that included the Representatives' Chamber so fatal to the hopes of William Morris Hunt. Finally, in 1877, the brownstone Gothic Episcopal cathedral of Garden City, Long Island, was begun, an edifice that was to have but little honor in the future despite its great spire and the lavish use of marble inside. Much of this work was quite good, but good in a mid-Victorian way that exaggerated the individual design elements rather than attempting, as was the case in the home, to blend them into a unified, somewhat plastic whole.

In the 1880s, Richardson Romanesque became a formidable rival of Gothic for churches. Gothic seemed to demand buttresses, pinnacles, towers—insistent verticals and irregularities of perimeter out of keeping with the plain, spreading, low-walled preaching spaces that were usually required. Romanesque, on the contrary, could dispense with the gesture of a tower if the congregation so wished, yet gain a fine effect through great roofs, a few doorways and large windows, and a few small-scaled, rippling arcades. If not quite so functional an enclosure of a great space as a trolley barn, such a church still represents a more rational and economical housing of a preaching space than a convincingly Gothic counterpart.

In the eighties, two cathedral competitions were held. Richardson and a recent arrival from England, Robert W. Gibson, were asked in 1882 to submit competing plans for the Episcopal cathedral at Albany. Richardson's designs were a sort of compromise between Romanesque and Gothic, with recognizable paraphrases of Notre-Dame and Chartres; Gibson's, which were adopted were in a fairly accomplished English Victorian Gothic.[85] In 1889, a much more important competition was held, this time for the Episcopal cathedral of St. John the Divine in New York.[86] Sixty designs, Gothic, Romanesque, and even early Renaissance, were submitted. The winners were George L. Heins and, more importantly, C. Grant LaFarge, son of John LaFarge. Their cathedral was to be Romanesque, outside, with some touches of Gothic; inside, it was to be, like Trinity, Boston, a "color church," a mixture of Romanesque and Byzantine. Construction was to be of solid masonry, and there were, possibly for the first time in America, to be calculated irregularities in plan and elevation to create a visually stimulating experience for the visitor as he moved through the great church. The length was to be 520 feet, about the length of Canterbury, and over a crossing 96 feet square was to rise a great spired tower about 500 feet high. This extremely ambitious project, to stand on a wooded bluff overlooking Harlem, was realized only in part. The rough masonry of the choir was erected, and work begun on the seven ambulatory "chapels of the tongues," dedicated to the component nations of the New York population. The structural skeleton of the crossing—dramatic late Victorian engineering masonry—was set up, while the crossing itself was covered with a "temporary" Guastavino dome that is still in place. Then, toward 1910, first Heins, then Bishop Potter, the sponsor of the work, died, and the commission was taken away from LaFarge. Stylistically, the design had become hopelessly out of date; since 1892, when work began, Gothic had been rejuvenated and was again a living style (Figs. 91, 92).[87]

Cram

LaFarge's successor at St. John's was the man most responsible for the revitalization of Gothic, Ralph Adams Cram (1863–1942).[88] Despite a very considerable amount of worldly success, Cram retained to the end of his life a quixotry that made him one of the characters of American architecture. It was not that he was eccentric; indeed, confronted with Cram, the modern world probably seemed aberrant. But he was a latter-day Pugin, who dreamed of a world where, under the eye of God, an aristocratic society, maintained by conscientious and contented workers, would flourish. Under Gothic vaults God would be glorified in stone and song, colored glass and fine joinery, vestments and precious metals. Christian gentlemen would be formed in the halls and cloisters of prep schools and universities, and here too the style would, in general, be Gothic. The home itself would be almost a sacramental institution, and its style would be one of the fine old styles of its region. Those in positions of power would acknowledge their responsibility, and those not in power, well looked after, would give of their best. Just as, in the church, all the arts, including the fine old Catholic ritual, would be united in the praise of God, so art and society in a world free of error would be united to inspire one another.[89]

When, as a teenager, Cram fell in with the mild but earnest bohemia of Boston in the 1880s, he already had a predisposition toward such attitudes, and a trip to Italy confirmed them. An encounter with a young American in Rome—providentially arranged, Cram was inclined to think—led him to attend a Christmas Eve midnight mass; there he had a powerful experience, the religious and aesthetic components of which he never seems to have attempted to separate, that caused him to join "the Anglican Communion of the Catholic Church." On the same trip, after seeing Palermo, Monreale, and finally Venice, he determined to be an architect. He opened his office in 1890, and a combination of forces soon led him to specialize in churches.

Most church architecture of the time, he felt, was simply not good enough—disunified, ill-calculated for its site, meretricious, filled with unsightly commercial furnishings and decoration. His first impulse was simply to take up English Gothic where it had stopped when Henry VIII suppressed the monasteries—not to turn back the clock so much as to set a much finer clock ticking again without readjusting the hands. Certain recent English Gothicists, including Henry Vaughan, who did a certain amount of work in the United States including the design for the National Cathedral in Washington, showed him the way. He went to the old English parish church for much of his inspiration and developed, after modern English precedent, a more massive, hall-like church for the city. He examined the plan of the Episcopal church and revised it with a hopeful eye toward High Church ritual, not in much favor then. (In a late work, the huge East Liberty Presbyterian Church [Fig. 93], he did the same, with the tacit consent of the Mellon donor; he noted that "it is a simple fact that, in half an hour, by the addition of a Crucifix and six candles on the Communion table, the church could be prepared for a pontifical High Mass, either of the Roman or the Anglican Rite.")[90] And he looked for, and encouraged, the artists and craftsmen whom he could regard as his peers in the search for perfection.

Tudor Gothic did not by itself satisfy him for long. He looked to earlier English Gothic, to continental Gothic—the Spanish was a special revelation—to Romanesque, to Spanish Renaissance and even Baroque, and to Colonial and Early Federal, which he often used for academic buildings and for "Protestant," as opposed to High Episcopalian, churches. When Roman Catholics, long retrograde architecturally, came to him for churches, he was delighted, and when Presbyterians, Methodists, and others, becoming more ritualistic, began to demand Gothic, he yielded with good grace.

Over the years, he propagandized; probably no other Eclectic wrote half as much. He wrote about the church building, from country chapel to cathedral, and what it should be; about how wonderful medieval life and architecture were (provoking some savage reviewing in the process); about the way the world should rebuild after the Great War; about the beautiful but little-known cathedral of Palma; and about his own life. He got involved in a variety of activities: the introduction of carol-singing in the streets of Beacon Hill; a project for "St. Botolph's Island," to be created in the middle of the Charles as an Ile de la Cité for Boston; the founding of the Medieval Academy of America; the commercial publication of *Mont Saint-Michel and Chartres*.

The output of his office, with its changing partners (and names) was tremendous. To mention a few: important additions to West Point; the completion (on paper) of St. John the Divine; the Swedenborgian cathedral at Bryn Athyn, Pa. (Fig. 94); the plan of St. Thomas', New York; the Graduate School and Chapel at Princeton; buildings at Williams, Wellesley, and Sweetbriar; at Philips Exeter and other prep schools (Fig. 95); the first parts of Rice University (Fig. 96); and especially many, many churches.

(*40*)

Goodhue

In the mid-nineties Cram took on a partner, Bertram Grosvenor Goodhue (1869–1924), who shared his romanticism and love of medieval splendor but had rather more artistic talent (Fig. 97).[91] Cram, on his own admission, was better at planning and general composition than at detailing, while Goodhue was extremely gifted at the latter. He was, in fact, a Gothic Stanford White, who could use old styles but somehow make them feel personal and contemporary. The New York churches that were his or largely his, especially St. Thomas' in elevation, St. Vincent Ferrer (Fig. 98), and St. Bartholomew's (Fig. 99), show him playing off masses against masses and verticals against horizontals with enormous skill and verve. But Gothic alone was not enough for Goodhue. He tried his hand at Churrigueresque in California (Fig. 100),[92] and the simpler Spanish styles as well. At the National Academy of Sciences he used a style half ancient Greek, half Greek Revival. And he began as well to look for something striking but beyond the historic styles. He experimented with tile mosaics on a grand scale, for vaults and domes over monumental interior spaces and for roofs and domes —following a Mexican precedent—outside. In the Los Angeles Public Library, though there was a hint of the Southwest mission church in the wall treatment, he was looking toward new forms, as he was also in his buildings for Cal Tech at Pasadena. And in his unexecuted design for the War Memorial in Kansas City and the state capitol at Lincoln, Nebraska (Fig. 101), he departed from style altogether. In these buildings he and his favorite sculptor Lee Lawrie worked out on a grand scale a scheme already used on the front of St. Vincent Ferrer, one in which buttress-like masses terminated, not in pinnacles or copings, but in human figures that grew out of the architectonic mass, becoming more organic and less planar, from bottom to top. By later standards, Goodhue was not a modernist. Whether he built in steel or masonry, the result was masonry. And there was no avant-grade elimination of decorative art: the art had somewhat new forms, that was all. The Convocation Building in New York, an unrealized project of his last years, had vast and patently impossible Gothic arches as major design elements of what would have been a very tall skyscraper.

Goodhue also produced a considerable amount of graphic art. He left architectural fantasies of the Near East in water color; Dürer-esque line drawings; fine pen renderings (Fig. 102); book designs, like those of the Kelmscott Press; bookplates; and several alphabets (Cheltenham, a standard display typeface, is a much-altered version of a Goodhue alphabet).

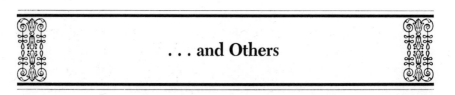

. . . and Others

Cram and Goodhue were the supreme figures of Eclectic Gothicism, but there were other skilled, even brilliant Gothicists who used other styles at times.[93] Maginnis and Walsh did good Gothic and Romanesque work for Catholic clients. James Gamble Rogers designed the theatrically beautiful Harkness Memorial complex at Yale (Fig. 103). Cope and Stewardson of Philadelphia first put into effect Princeton's policy of 1896 of building henceforth in Gothic with some very handsome Tudor work; they designed Tudor and Jacobean at Bryn Mawr College, Jacobean at Washington University, St. Louis, and, in a more cheerful red-and-white, at Penn (Fig. 104); and ventured into unrelated styles—Colonial at Haverford College, François I for a Philadelphia office building, Mexican Baroque for a school for the blind in suburban Philadelphia. Another Philadelphia office, Day and Klauder (and later, Charles Z. Klauder by himself), showed an even finer hand with academic Gothic: the Freshman dormitories at Princeton, the Peabody Museum and power house at Yale, and the preposterous but beautifully detailed Cathedral of Learning in Pittsburgh (Fig. 105). Klauder was gifted in other styles, too: witness a Christian Science church in Philadelphia, like a large semi-rustic version of the Pazzi Chapel, and a splendid Georgian double range at the University of Delaware.[94]

Commercial Gothic

Gothic was never terribly popular for commercial architecture, and yet there were attempts to use it, especially for very tall buildings where classic horizontality presented problems, and two of the most famous skyscrapers of the Eclectic period were in the style. The first was the Woolworth Building by Cass Gilbert, completed in 1913 (Figs. 106, 107). Flemish Gothic realized in cream-colored terra cotta, it stressed the vertical with hardly a dissenting line. In place of cornices, it used ogival lambrequins, slightly projecting like the canopies of choir stalls, and a shaft rose from lower, much broader, masses: it seemed, indeed, to anticipate the Zoning Law of three years later.

The second was the Chicago Tribune Building by Hood and Howells, winners of an open competition in 1922 (Fig. 108). Like that for St. John the Divine, the Tribune competition served to take the pulse of the profession—in this case, of the profession in Europe as well as America.[95] Gropius, Dudok, Loos (whose submission was a titanic, fenestrated, Doric column), Bivoet and Duiker, and Eliel Saarinen were among the foreigners. Goodhue submitted a massive tower, slightly diminished at the top and with some polychrome inlay effects that won imitative attention. Hood and Howells' design was in a polished, rather academic, Gothic, owing much to the Tour de Beurre of Rouen Cathedral.

The Romantic Suburb

Beyond the formal Gothic of church, school, and business building, that might be called classically romantic, lay the more amorphous romanticism of the suburban house. By 1920 it was no longer fashionable for a family, as it were, to wear all its jewels at once. A rambling Tudor house, for example, with a grandiose homeyness about it, executed in a painterly mixture of fieldstone, imitation-adzed half-timber, and artfully variegated and rough-edged slates with exposed surfaces diminished from eaves to ridge in the Old English manner, came to seem more desirable. The less wealthy favored a Cotswold cottage, a modest stuccoed Italian villa that might have urns on the gate piers and *putti* over the front door, or a fragment of a Norman farmhouse or chateau with a great hipped roof. Because Colonial and Early Federal (or Early Republican, in the parlance of the twenties), were classical, they represented exceptions, though very popular ones, to the prevailing romanticism (Fig. 109). Often virtuously humble affairs of shutters and pent eaves, they sometimes appeared in a more august mode that was, however, conceived as a stately minuet rather than as a Baroque fanfare.

As the suburbs expanded, so did the specialized suburban house practice. Feeding on the increasing number of books of photographs and sketches of vernacular architecture in England, Spain, France, and Italy, and of folio monographs on other contemporary suburban architects, offices in each American city turned out house after house, which, if the architects had the right touch, looked like soft-pencil sketches or watercolors rather than houses (Fig. 110). They were not so much houses as three-dimensional pictures of Homes, in each of which A Family dwelt, in contentment, among the maples and rhododendrons.

The Philadelphia area was especially blessed with fine residential architecture. Until the 1880s practitioners such as Samuel Sloan and Frank Furness had dominated the scene with designs that were good but that had, in full measure, the mid-Victorian hardness; Furness was, and remains, famous for a strident Gothic mannerism.[96] In 1881, though, the Aesthetic movement found a highly talented exponent in Wilson Eyre (1858–1944), who in his long career figured as the architectural counterpart of the early "Brandywine tradition"—the Howard Pyle, the Maxfield Parrish, of architecture, combining the love of fantasy and the sophisticated simplification that were also twin strains in the graphic arts around the turn of the century.[97] With Eyre started the gentle whimsy that has characterized much Philadelphia architecture since, up to, and including Venturi (Fig. 111–

114). A school of architects followed him, specializing in residential architecture and taking advantage of the lovely, silver-gray "Wissahickon schist" and other ledge stones of the region to produce Colonial, Cotswold, and less readily categorized buildings for Chestnut Hill and the other tree-shaded neighborhoods around Philadelphia (Figs. 115–118).[98]

The suburb did not, of course, consist solely of houses. There was, almost by definition, a railroad station or at least a string of trolley shelters, and there were shops, libraries, schools, and churches. The churches were, as a rule, Gothic or Colonial, and in them a certain provincial grandeur was not out of place; the same was true of the high school and the public library. As new buildings replaced the cranky vernacular ones of the original village, though, the architects usually strove for an idealized, possibly Europeanized, village atmosphere, sometimes in a mildly new style, as in Grosvenor Atterbury's station square for Forest Hills Gardens, but usually in Tudor or Colonial. The station, whose appearance might result from tactful negotiation with the railroad, was often in a vaguely Norman Farmhouse, or at least rustic, style.

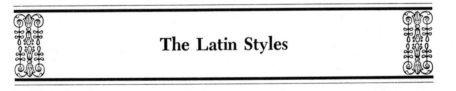

The Latin Styles

But there were parts of the country where the Anglo-Saxon heritage was not supreme, particularly in areas settled first by Latins: California, the Southwest, Louisiana, and Florida.[99] In California, the Mission Style existed already at the turn of the century, and more elaborate Spanish architecture, larded with Moorish and Meso-American motifs, followed (Figs. 119, 120). In Florida, Spanish flourished also, thanks to Addison Mizner and others who were hard at work during the great land boom of the 1920s (Fig. 121).[100] Here, however, the presence of so much water, a selling point, suggested the introduction of Venetian Gothic, and the two

Mediterranean styles lived side by side. In Louisiana a Hispano-French style, partly inspired by the Vieux Carré, partly by the raised hip-roofed plantation houses of the pre-Greek Revival period, came into being. In New Mexico, the Pueblo Style, reminiscent of adobe building, was used by Rapp and Rapp and other local offices, to produce soft-cornered structures with battered walls and wobbly parapets, with what seemed to be *canales* and the ends of *vigas* protruding from them (Fig. 122).[101]

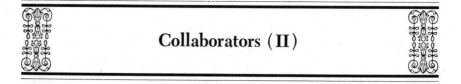

Collaborators (II)

The figurative arts remained active participants in the grander designs. As the Beaux-Arts influence died away the grand parade of allegorical sculpture and fresco tapered off but certainly did not stop. Heroic allegory, though, became only one manner among several. Theaters, restaurants, and commercial buildings, though a shade more solid and solemn than they had been around 1910, were decorated increasingly with themes of Italian gardens, forest glades, carnivals, or harbors and industry—places and occasions dedicated to the creation of wealth or the enjoyment of leisure. With artists like Frank Brangwyn and Barry Faulkner the painter's treatment became more impressionistic and the palette more brilliant—or at least not so dark and powerfully modeled as it had been with Blashfield and Cox. Sculpture became more stylized, less concerned with anatomy and clothing and more with a lively summing-up of the figure. Lee Lawrie, as we have seen, collaborated with Goodhue in fusing architecture and sculpture. Paul Manship kept the figure intact but so stylized that it tended to become abstract.

This, at least, is the way things were in secular architecture. Church architecture was another matter. Here, the problem was to catch the spirit of, and to match in excellence, the medieval masters.[102] Secular, classically oriented architecture had its own decorum but offered the artist more freedom, more neutral space in which his work could display itself. In the church, a statue had to be put in a narrow niche, or a stained-glass cartoon adapted to a tracery design and an iconographic program (Figs. 123, 124). The artists who worked for Cram, Goodhue, and the other church architects and were thus subordinated to architecture and iconography have perhaps deservedly become obscure figures. How many historians of twentieth-century art have ever heard the names of John Angel, sculptor of the baptistry and the western doors of St. John the Divine, or I. Kirchmayer, the woodcarver Cram praised so highly? In Church circles Charles Connick is known because his stained-glass studio is still active, and perhaps another artist in stained glass, Nicola D'Ascenzo, as well. Samuel Yellin is remembered by a few veterans of the old architectural offices, but how much Yellin ironwork is rescued from the smelter when a church goes down? Cram envisioned a place of worship where the arts would gather, but how much of the art, except perhaps the church building itself, has received any serious attention outside narrow ecclesiastical circles since 1940? Today, the church artists of the Eclectic period are merely a subject for an *ubi sunt*: but who can say that a new way of seeing will not come, when art lovers will make Eclectic church crawls to inspect pulpits and stained glass? (There always have been guided tours of many such churches, let us remember.) Or was their art all stillborn, never really enjoyed, or too strictly of its time to be meaningful now?[103]

The role of the building industry as the architect's helper had been developing steadily during the early Eclectic period. A good plasterer could trowel in a half-dozen ways to give the proper textural effects for each style. Artfully chipped slates, skintled bricks, and purposefully warped roofing tiles were available for the romantic suburban house. Samples of brickwork, laid in mortar and bound up in metal straps, lay about in architects' offices, and swatches of stone arrived in the mail. Materials manufacturers and their trade associations put out elaborate books of "precedents" (i.e., buildings and details to imitate). The American Face Brick Association, for instance, published *Brickwork in Italy* (1925), which covered the subject from the ancient Romans to around 1910, and *English Precedent for Modern Brickwork* (1924). Weyerhaeuser Company published the White Pine Monographs, devoted to Colonial and Early Federal architecture where wood was important, with drawings suggesting modern detailing (Fig. 125), and the Ludowici-Celadon Company, tilemakers, put out the Tuileries Brochures to tempt architects to use their Imperial Roofing Tile—actually rustic in effect—by offering photographs and measured drawings of English and French architecture that might look well if roofed in Imperial Tile.[104] The makers of prefabricated ornament continued to issue catalogues of their stock that allowed pragmatic designers of commercial space to sprinkle rosettes and festoons over the bare structure in the design of which their real talents lay (Fig. 126).

The Grandeur of the State

The architecture of the various federal, state, county, and municipal governments was an affair somewhat apart.[105] Though other styles were used at times, especially in the late Victorian period, monumental classicism was always regarded as proper for any official building larger than a village hall, and formulas were early adapted or invented that persisted through the 1930s despite the decline of Eclecticism in all other areas of American architecture. The Second Empire style, along with the Italianate, surviving from the 1850s, had persisted well into the Aesthetic period. This, around 1870, was complemented but not ousted by Gothic, which left one major monument, Upjohn's state capitol at Hartford, finished in 1878. Queen Anne was influential in county courthouse design in the 1880s, and the construction of the Allegheny County Courthouse in Pittsburgh, finished in 1888, made Richardson Romanesque perhaps the most fashionable style into the mid-nineties for city halls, courthouses, and post offices. Thereafter classicism, whether modestly Colonial, austerely Roman, or lavishly Beaux-Arts, dominated official architecture for almost fifty years (Fig. 127).[106] Many of the official buildings in the major cities presented the same problem that the United Nations complex would later on—monumental treatment of buildings in which office space bulked far larger than grand interiors. In essence, a federal building, county courthouse, or even city hall, located in a big city was an office building, but without ground-floor shops and only a few stories high. A fairly obvious classical formula was usually adapted to the problem; on a massive basement, often heavily rusticated, half-columns or pilasters rose for three or four stories to support an entablature; above this, half-hidden by the cornice, might be an attic. (Private institutions sometimes used this formula as well.)[107] Sited at one end of an enclosed open space of the right size, as Gilbert's New York Custom House is on Bowling Green, such a building could be quite handsome. Often, however, because of their enclosed look, their superhuman scale, their artificiality of design, and their somber materials—gray granite quite often—such buildings look self-centered and aloof, mere voids in the busy street scene. Business buildings, even banks, have an air of welcome and life that these pompous nests of officials almost totally lack; they are, as a whole, one of Eclecticism's great failures. Later examples, as we shall see below, came under the influence of the skyscraper.

Apart from such buildings, the architecture of each level of government conformed more or less to a special self-image. The federal government in Washington was, of course, very correctly classical, whether as in the Senate and House office buildings of Carrère and Hastings, graciously and delicately eighteenth-century French, or as in the simpler but very massive buildings of the Federal Triangle, executed in the thirties by a number of collaborating firms. The Supreme Court building of 1935, by Cass Gilbert's office, is overblown but archaeologically correct Roman (Fig. 128), and Pope's National Archives building of the same year is a giant coffer, not very pleasant inside, and owing something of its exterior to St. George's Hall in Liverpool. In other Washington buildings constructed under federal auspices but not used for government business, classicism is again strong. The Lincoln Memorial of 1922, by Henry Bacon (1866–1924), is a neoclassic temple, combining a Grecian Doric order with an attic in a design of such excellence that perhaps only Frank Lloyd Wright has fully succeeded in despising it (Fig. 129). By 1939, when the National Gallery and the Jefferson Memorial (Fig. 130), both by Pope, were undertaken, a greater simplicity may have seemed advisable; yet both monuments, for all their fine materials and grand scale, are not so much austere as negative; since there were to be cornices, one feels that they should have had more of an air of conviction about them.

In the place where the citizen most commonly encounters the federal government—the post office—a wider variety of styles was practiced, from the Imperial Roman colossus that McKim, Mead and White erected in New York in 1913 to the pleasant Colonial and Greek Revival offices for the small towns and suburbs of the 1930s.

The state capitol usually had a dome, or something suggesting a dome; otherwise, it was a special variety of the official office building, extended into wings to suggest bicamerality rather than being cubed into a box.[108] Classicism was common but not inevitable. Gilbert's Minnesota capitol of 1896–1905 (Fig. 131) and the roughly contemporary Pennsylvania capitol (begun 1902) were heavily Renaissance, with domes after St. Peter's, but Goodhue's Nebraska capitol (begun 1922) is in the free style that he was developing before his death, while the Oregon capitol of much later (begun 1936) has a slotted drum on a Modernistic body and the North Dakota capitol (begun 1933), like the United Nations complex, allows the offices to tower over the legislative chambers.

The courthouses of rural counties, once Romanesque was out of vogue, were almost always classical, and often Beaux-Arts. Seldom designed by architects of any sophistication, they held on to faded compositional formulas and treatments, loosely interpreted.

City halls differed widely. The Victorian, French-inspired system of pavilions and a tower was dropped as the number of desk personnel grew, and when the Nebraska capitol, its central tower surrounded by a spreading mass of public spaces, was finished a number of cities emulated it. Municipal towers arose in the late twenties that gave sphygmomanometric testimony to the pressure of public business, and perhaps such towers, not too different from those of office buildings, were supposed to be an assurance to the public that the city government was being run with businesslike efficiency (Fig. 132). Some of the stylistic daring of the commercial skyscraper was apparent, and a modernized classicism, or classicized Modernistic, appeared fairly often. Courthouses, county and federal, used this formula too. Village halls, on the other hand, were as a rule Colonial, Tudor, Norman Farmhouse, or Spanish well into the thirties, as were police stations and firehouses.

Apogee

In the later 1920s three surveys of American architecture appeared, all written from the Eclectic viewpoint. These were Talbot Hamlin's *The American Spirit in Architecture,* Thomas Tallmadge's *The Story of Architecture in America,* and G. H. Edgell's *The American Architecture of To-day.* All three writers were happy about the state of American architecture in their time and optimistic about the future. Since 1870 the architectural profession had gained in knowledge, wisdom, and polish; the lessons of the past had been well learned, and yet had not stunted the creative growth of really good architects. There had been interesting experiments in composition and ornament, and that new beauty had sometimes resulted was not denied. There was no grudging of praise for Sullivan as an ornamentalist, for instance, and the mountainlike post-1916 skyscraper was acknowledged to be a vital addition to the architecture of the country. And yet, though there was mild disapproval of "archaeological" designs, a general feeling is apparent that the historic styles, however simplified and modified, were still, for a while, best for the traditional institutions of society, the home, the church, and the school. If there was to be an evolution in the architecture of these structures out of the old styles into new ones, it had best be a slow and careful one.

As it happens, the evolution never occurred. On paper, at least, an intolerant, war-of-religion spirit divided the profession into two camps around 1930, each denouncing the other as shallow and dishonest: a reflection of something that had happened in the figurative arts at least as early as the Armory Show. Modernism—and here we mean only a determined abstinence from historic forms—was no monolithic movement that came over from Europe in 1928 or that erupted from the American soil to present a united, impenetrable front to the Eclectics. It included both lovers of rugged, atavistic stone and timber and those who could see no valid architecture except in pure arrangements of white cement, steel, and large sheets of glass. The sole thread that bound these innovators together was a desire to realize, belatedly and against odds, a range of architectural forms appropriate to varying conditions of twentieth-century

America. Eclecticism was hedonistic, self-indulgent, recognizing as guiding principles only beauty of a well-understood kind, and the appropriateness of the style of a building to its function (you could almost jumble Sullivan, Buffon, and MacLuhan and say that under Eclecticism the style *was* the function).

At the height of Eclecticism—witness the example of Goodhue—an architectural office might favor a certain style and yet venture into other styles, nonhistoric ones included, as the occasion seemed to dictate. Bernard Maybeck was extravagantly and lyrically Beaux-Arts at the Panama-Pacific Exposition, but Gothic or Spanish on many other occasions, and withal modern enough that he has continued to be respected. John Russell Pope, a very cool classicist indeed in his best-known work, produced in the Stuart Duncan house at Newport a grand and tasteful Tudor mansion, while his own house in that town is excruciatingly quaint. Cass Gilbert, whose best-known building is Gothic and whose work was generally Beaux-Arts or of some more restrained form of classicism, designed the functionalistic Army Supply Base in Brooklyn, a study in poured concrete reduced to pier and mullions, of which he was proud and which won critical praise in its time (Fig 133). On the other hand, Ely Jacques Kahn, a modernist specializing in office and loft buildings, abandoned his usual Art Deco-Modernistic manner when he built the Glen Oaks Country Club, at Great Neck, in an Early Federal style.

The office of Albert Kahn of Detroit (1869–1942) suggests the range of commissions one Eclectic firm undertook.[109] Beginning with Mason and Rice, a good early Eclectic office, Kahn set out on his own not long before the automobile industry became important. His brother Julius, his office engineer, invented a greatly improved system of concrete reinforcement around 1905, and from then on Kahn's office had a twofold role: on the one hand, it produced polished Eclectic work in a variety of styles—some of the best done in the teens and twenties (Fig. 134)—and on the other, industrial buidings of such simple elegance that Kahn is best remembered outside Detroit as an outstanding American modernist.

The feeling one gets, then, is that the architects who led the profession around 1920, the most intelligent or at least the most literate of the lot, were far from being bound to one manner. However much they might love Renaissance or Gothic they could "do" some other style when they saw good reason for doing so, even if that style was a newly invented one. Gilbert's warehouses for the Army seemed to call for a new style, or non-style, and he supplied it. The skyscraper made a similar demand, much more often and much more publicly. So did the powerhouse, the factory, and quite a few other modern buildings, and a look at these structures, which by their very natures pressured architects toward modernism, will be useful at this point. We must remember that such places were the tools of modern business and technology, with new and extraordinary demands in the way of scale, proportions, fenestration, and so on, and that they had no old and strong traditions to dictate composition or ornament. If the Eclectics produced solutions for such problems not to be pedigreed in Bannister Fletcher or Speltz, this did not in the least imply that their next church would not be Colonial or their next mansion Tudor, or that they would not fall to these more traditional problems with a will. Thus, their modernism was different from that of those who called for a total and complete abolition of the Styles.[110]

The Post-1916 Skyscraper

The Zoning Law of 1916, we repeat, imposed a ziggurat-plus-tower form on the New York skyscraper and suppressed its cornices.[111] Gothicism seemed to show the way to a new solution for a while, but despite the Woolworth and the Tribune buildings it soon lost its popularity. One probable explanation was scale plus economics. The lambrequins of the Woolworth Building were a little too small to be effective, and more recent legislation would probably have had the effect of making them still smaller, or at least of preventing them from jutting far enough to cast a good shadow. The alternatives, if a skyscraper were to be Gothic, would be a crown of pinnacles and buttresses big enough to show up properly at several hundred yards' distance—an extravagance—or huge pointed arches that would necessarily curtail light in several stories and would probably demand a filling of tracery—a worse extravagance.[112] And even were these sacrifices to be made, they were solutions that operated in spite of, rather than through, the stepped-back masses.

In the mid-1920s, in New York, traditionalists felt that the Shelton Hotel by Arthur Loomis Harmon (b. 1901) offered a better solution (Fig. 135).[113] Its basement was an outright masonry expression in Lombardic Romanesque, but from there upward it rose in masses of dark, rough brick—the texturalism of the suburbs had by this time invaded urban residential architecture of all heights—that were divided into piers and panels. The central tower ended in simple tracery, some fretwork beneath the parapet, and a hipped tiled roof. The building thus had a dark, sullen power that was much admired; the brutal scale of the city, its heaving-up of inhabited masses, had become the stuff of romance, and the Shelton seemed to respond to this romance without casting off tradition altogether.

The problem with the Shelton (the expense of the pier-and-panel system and the ornament aside) was the fact that it was a hotel—no massed battalions of office workers needing maximum light and air, but perhaps two people to share each window. The masses could be truly massive, with twice as much wall in plan as window (Fig. 136).

A more promising solution for the office skyscraper was the second-prize submission to the Tribune competition. Eliel Saarinen (1873–1950) was still practicing in Finland when he created this work, which to many American architects *really* solved the problem (Fig. 137). Here, above an arcuated base that still looks like masonry, a screen of glass and close-set mullions rises between flanking bastions—which also look like masonry—until at last they rise free, returned at their ends to form reentering angles with their counterparts on the other three fronts. These are stepped back twice, and at last a ribbed, gently modeled tower rises to a predetermined point, then stops without any final gesture. The steel cage of horizontal cells is buried; instead, there is a strong feeling of something rising, and becoming richer and lighter as it ascends. This theme of rising piers, topped by neither pinnacles nor cornice, was rapidly adopted, as was the motif of narrow round-arched windows hinting that a certain zone of the composition was being terminated. In Detroit, the offices of Albert Kahn Associates and Smith, Hinchman and Grylls, both very Eclectic in the twenties, did several tall buildings that owe much to Saarinen.[114] In San Francisco, Miller and Pfleuger's Pacific Telephone Building finished with a flourish of stepped-back piers and mullions, and so, in a more powerful way, did Sloan and Robertson's Chanin Building in New York. These are but a few examples of the influence of the Finnish architect.

For that matter, Raymond Hood (1881–1934) and John Mead Howells (b. 1868), the Tribune competition winners, seemed also to have profited from Saarinen. Hood's American Radiator Building in New York, finished in 1924, began by stylizing Flamboyant Gothic and realizing it in a deep brown brick ending in an ornate crown touched up in gold—thus starting a vogue for "black-and-gold" office buildings. By 1930 Hood had carried the verticality all the way in the New York Daily News Building, with its piers of white brick, totally unadorned, embracing unframed windows and spandrel panels of russet terra cotta (Fig. 138). His other work of the late twenties is so varied that one recent history petulantly calls him facile. He created Modernistic interiors that threatened to roast the eyeballs; a household appliance store with a giant refrigerator on top; a Modernistic house painted in a pastel version of dazzle camouflage; and, at the same time, the modernized yet very fancy Gothic of the Scottish Rite Cathedral at Scranton, Pennsylvania. Howells, older and more traditional, made few "statements," but his Panhellenic Hotel of 1930, again in New York, combined the massiveness of the Shelton with the jetting verticality of Saarinen's design and was justly admired.[115]

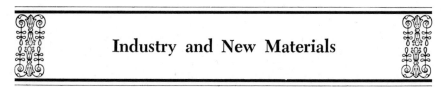

Industry and New Materials

That a commercial building should cast off tradition and look venturesome was of course reasonable. (Banks, naturally enough, were a holdout: a bank should not look too speculative [Fig. 139].) It was no less reasonable that a powerhouse, a waterworks, a warehouse, or any other conspicuous but culturally extraneous building in the community should do the same. Such buildings could be treated according to a traditional formula, and often were; until

1915 or so, the powerhouse was almost always a titanic orangery, and the warehouse might be an orangery with blind windows (Fig. 140). But no one appears to have felt passionately, at any time, that they *should* be so treated, and so these too became subjects for at least mild experimentation. (An exception, here, was the electrical substation; when placed in a residential area, it was often treated, or disguised, in a traditional manner intended to be "harmonious.")

The factory and the loft building were more difficult problems. After 1910, they were reinforced-concrete cages, filled with the very maximum amount of glass in most of their panels. Engineers who felt the need to qualify this starkness in some way floundered, all too obviously. Certain city buildings, such as department stores, small office buildings, and automobile salesrooms, clad their similar cagework in ornate cream terra-cotta or tapestry brick, but the cages of industry, either for economy's sake or because of their less desirable locations, compromised either with a blatantly false front (usually classical) with no architectural treatment whatever behind or with a few bits of traditional ornament, a cornice included, scattered over the meager solid areas. The cage pattern was too strong to permit any real success with traditional forms, however, and a sort of free style, using inlays of tile and slightly fanciful parapets, became the expedient way out. Little of this, old or new in style, was very satisfactory.[116]

Then there were concourses, subway stations, the low platform shelters that were the successors of the Victorian train sheds, and later on the bus stations and airport buildings: areas where people were on the move, where easy circulation and maintenance were important, and where plans and proportions were hostile to traditional compositions. Ceramic, concrete, and steel were the materials used in such places, and though the exteriors might be treated in a traditional style, the newness of the program invited, and often got, a new approach.[117]

Even new decorative materials suggested new forms. This was particularly true of earth materials. "Tapestry" brick, which came into use some time before 1910, gave the architect a large range of shades and colors to chose from in a ruggedly textured brick, either of normal proportions or elongated like Roman brick. By preference tapestry brick was laid up in thick mortar, often mixed with an aggregate of small pebbles so that a rich, variegated surface resulted. Fancy bonds were often used to create panels in the areas of plain wall, and inlays of tile at accented points were often used as substitutes for the usual carved and molded ornament. Terra-cotta also flourished. *Brickbuilder*, a magazine reviewing architecture in baked-earth materials, held competitions that encouraged the lavish use of terra-cotta as well as brick, and from about 1905 on terra-cotta appeared in prize-winning designs with increased freedom and flamboyance. It remains to be seen whether it influenced or reflected contemporary work in commercial and theater architecture, sometimes equally uninhibited in dabbling with nonhistoric treatments. Concrete, still used more often around 1905 in inert masses than as material in tension, cried out for "treatment" while resisting obvious attempts to turn it into a limestone substitute. Variations on the Doric order, pseudo-rustication, and so on were common enough, but some considered the inherent shapeless massiveness of concrete and its latent texture as promising bases for experimentation and, like Wright at Unity Temple, washed the surfaces freed from the formwork with acid to expose the aggregate or nailed moldings inside the formwork itself to shape it in new, simple forms. Steelwork, we have already said, was half-heartedly tamed when close to the public eye.

The modernists, of course, affected to believe that the new constructional methods and materials should be used "frankly," and regarded any attempt to cover or coax them into conformity with the Styles as dishonest, and therefore bad, architecture. Their basic theory is appealing: let the steelwork, the reinforced concrete, of the bridge, the skyscraper, the factory show forth unadorned; let the strong clean lines establish new, vital, and primitive forms for architecture, even as polished machine parts might evoke new forms in sculpture. If there was strength in these things, why shy away from them merely because of the newness of their forms?[118]

As we have seen, though, engineering is indifferent to geometrical elegance; an expedient balance of performance, time, and money is what counts. The bridge that creeps across the river on bents is usually cheaper and quicker to build than one that takes the void in one flying leap; the concrete cage of the factory may be beset with ramps, brick superstructures, and proliferating ductwork; for that matter, not all machinery surfaces were presentable, around 1930, at the Museum of Modern Art. Functional beauty, then, is an occasional coincidence in modern engineering (and often due to the hand of the industrial designer) rather than the necessary result of letting the engineer have his own way. To obtain that beauty infallibly, artistic judgment, not severe practicality, is needed.

Moreover, architecture—including that admired by *and* that produced by the modernists—has always presented an edited version of the constructional facts. Japanese frame architecture, seemingly so straightforward, abounds in small shams introduced for the sake of finish.[119] The Gothic cathedral dramatizes its structure with shafts, clustered around the piers, that support absolutely nothing and ribs that are often totally unnecessary.[120] Coming closer to home, Gropius and Le Corbusier finish off brick or rubble walls with white cement, as if to suggest concrete or some seamless industrially produced sheeting, while Wright pads out his Prairie House chimneys and reverses Corbusian practice by veneering the concrete walls of the Imperial Hotel in hand-made brick.[121]

The Eclectics, of course, deviated much farther from the realities of construction to attain preconceived effects, and often cultivated as well a deliberate archaism of materials and workmanship. Perhaps Geoffrey Scott offered them moral support (if they needed it) in the first instance.[122] And they probably regarded the rejection of machine-age resources, aesthetics aside, purely as an affair between the client and his bank account; if he, too, liked (and could afford) granite columns turned on giant lathes in Vermont, or Merrie English roofs of rough-edged slating diminished, course to course, from eaves to ridge, why force pilotis and asphalt on him? If the modernists believed in facing the facts (albeit with cement stucco or hand-made brick), the Eclectic wanted rather to create a pleasant experience, not without a gentle cultural message, in his buildings.

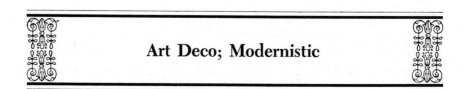

Art Deco; Modernistic

Art Deco, even Modernistic, had for the Eclectic an emulsifying function, allowing him to be "modern" without disorientation; not only were these styles fluid enough to be fitted to buildings of unprecedented dimensions and proportions, but they could retain the symmetry, the density and placing of ornament, and the massing, derived from the masonry tradition, that he was used to.[123]

What we now know as Art Deco was formally introduced to the United States at the Exposition des Arts Decoratifs, held at Paris in 1925.[124] When Art Deco really arrived here, however, remains to be ascertained. Art Nouveau, its forerunner, had had a small vogue, and of course Louis Comfort Tiffany had even contributed to it. And it is reasonable to assume that some smart shops had always followed the latest French modes, even in their decoration. Some American architects, too, must have known about it already: one of the most distinguished buildings of the 1920s, the Barclay-Vesey Building of the New York Telephone Company, was finished in 1926 and already includes Art Deco ornament of stylized plant and animal motifs (Fig. 141). Nor was Paris a city exactly shunned by Americans in the 1920s in any case, and the prestige of its artists in the figurative arts, and of the Beaux-Arts for architecture, remained strong enough to draw American artists there—artists who could be inspired with new ideas as they passed through the streets, just as McKim had hoped Americans of a previous generation would be in Rome.

Client attitudes merit investigation at this point, too. The twenties was a peculiar decade, full of rigidity and revolt, and a yen for the new but not totally unfamiliar may have impelled young and monied clients (money buys cultural perspective along with other things) to look for the trendy, the brittle even, without casting off moorings to the past entirely. Much of what was "modern" around 1925 was not too different from some of the things Soane had done over a hundred years earlier, but the simplification of traditional motifs seemed new once again.

Art Deco, a nouveau-riche successor to Art Nouveau influenced by the less dense and more rectilinear avant-garde styles of Austria and Germany, came to America with its fountains, its superimposed blossoms, its symmetrically leaping impalas, and its stylized human figures about the time that the French themselves were moving into a more abstract, more geometrical manner. This quickly arrived too, was combined with American Indian motifs, suggestions from the works of Wright and a few followers in the twenties, and possibly from other sources, and evolved into the Modernistic. Lacking the stern intellectual and ethical bases of the modernism that was to triumph eventually, this new style still appealed to something in a good many young or middle-aged dwellers in the modern city. That Paul Frankl, a New York decorator, could design "skyscraper furniture" and label it as such in his books says much about a new sense of the meaningful in imagery in the late twenties. His *New Dimensions* of 1928 (with a dedication to, and vaguely friendly foreword by, Wright) shows only pieces of his own and a few other Americans, probably exhibited in department stores and museums (the Metropolitan was exhibiting contemporary decorative art), plus executed European interiors. His *Form and Re-Form* of 1930, however, can show real, executed, American examples, by Frankl himself, by William Lescaze, and by a number of others. It would be especially interesting to study the clients of the Modernistic designers, particularly those who commissioned them to decorate offices and apartments. One guesses that they were of early middle age, many Jewish or at least of recent immigrant stock, having no associative ties with Colonial or Tudor and happy to identify themselves with the perpetual prosperous immediacy, the jagged and geometrical skyline, of the hustling city where their fortunes were made. Modernistic speaks of New York, and in the illustrations of the attractively overdesigned pages of *Form and Re-Form*, after more than forty years, the pride of some New Yorkers, circa 1930, still shines (Fig. 142).

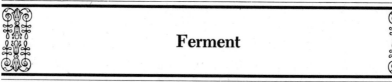

Ferment

If intelligent architects and critics in the mid-1920s hoped for a peaceful evolution away from the Styles, their hopes were soon dashed by a sequence of events.[125] 1927–28 was important for architectural modernism both in Europe and in the United States. Le Corbusier built his Villa Stein at Garches in 1927, and in the same year his double house at the Stuttgart Exhibition, an event that also saw important work by Gropius and Mies and that, some feel, was the place where the International Style crystallized out of the recently matured works of these architects. In the same year, *Vers une architecture* emerged in translation as *Towards a New Architecture*. In America, Neutra, not long in the United States, planned the Lovell "health" house, to be built over the next two years. Buckminster Fuller exhibited the first Dymaxion house. Norman Bel Geddes, a stage designer of avant-garde tendencies (stage design had to some extent conditioned audiences to new, stripped-down forms), became in 1927 one of the first industrial designers, possibly the first so to call himself. He was quickly followed by Raymond Loewy, Henry Dreyfuss, and others, coming from various disciplines.[126] This new profession was soon to challenge the architect and the engineer by shaping buildings as well as machines. The first American museum for avant-garde art, the Gallery of Living Art, was established in 1927, and in the same year Henry-Russell Hitchcock began to write and lecture on modern architecture,[127] while a "Machine-Age Exposition" of that year invited the public to see avant-garde architecture, art, and machine design together. In January 1928 Wright, presumed dead by some European critics, published once again in *Architectural Record*—a series called, like his *Record* articles of 1908 and 1914, "In the Cause of Architecture."[128]

Architects and fledgling architects were already in some sort of turmoil. Hitchcock reports that *Vers une architecture* was well known at the Harvard Graduate School even before it was translated, and the AIA Convention of 1927 was much, if dubiously, occupied with the question of modernism and what form it should take: evidence that the issue was already on everyone's mind. Doubtless there were innumerable drafting-room debates, and growing discontent in the schools with the standard academic problems, which were intended to create tasteful artists rather than practical planners or, for that matter, to cultivate brilliance in design.

Besides, some Eclectic work, even by widely respected architects, had obviously gone too far. That James Gamble Rogers, at Yale, should attack steps with grinding wheels to suggest centuries of plodding students was mere theatricalism, not architecture,[129] and that he should build a linking range of buildings with one façade Colonial and the other Gothic for harmony's sake was a little hard to take too. Even worse, that Pope should propose for this same romantic university a library whose reading room would be King's

College Chapel and whose bookstack would be a cathedral tower suggested an all-that-money-can-buy, Ghost-Goes-West mentality to be found as well in the contemporary importation of rooms, even whole buildings, from Europe by the wealthy (Figs. 143–145).[130] The growing passive reliance on old accomplishments around 1920, without any contribution of importance by the present-day architect, might have come to threaten the art of architecture itself.

Some time before 1930, the attitudes expressed in writing by Sullivan and Wright—total and contemptuous rejection of the Styles in contemporary architecture—began to appear in the writings of others. The nagging feeling that a distinctive new style should emerge had long been present, both in Europe and America, but without much being done about it. Architects in pattern books of the 1840s and 50s had included an "American" house now and then, even though the Persian villa a few pages on was also intended for America,[131] and *American Architect* in the late seventies had opened its pages for debate as to how the charming but macaronic domestic architecture of the Aesthetic period should evolve.[132] But the feeling circa 1928 was more than a mild longing for a new style. A stern judgment was laid upon those who had designed Eclectic architecture and those who had commissioned it. Art criticism will be the last stronghold of fanaticism when tolerance suffuses all other ramifications of the human condition, and it is not perhaps to be wondered that the lovers of pediments were now called hard names by a growing chorus, accused of immoralities various and sundry because they had not anticipated the writers' preferences. In the propaganda that began in earnest a little before 1930 and that is echoed in most subsequent histories of American architecture—history being written by the winning side—there was a strong ethical stress: Eclecticism was dishonest architecture for dishonest people—or if not dishonest, shallow, weak, sterile, negligible (Fig. 146).[133] Architect and client alike were accused of failing as human beings, all across the board, and of displaying an appalling lack of sensibility. There were even sexual overtones. "Modern" architecture has projected a virile image: engineers, machines, Chicago businessmen, pioneers, forthrightness, the West, unadorned brute structure, Whitman, Thoreau, nature, rugged materials, earth colors, etc. Eclecticism, with its delicate adjustments and its reverence for precedents, was made to seem squaw stuff by comparison, effluvia of the "shelter" magazines.[134]

Some Eclectics attempted to meet the new feeling partway, or had already been attempting compromises that would not tear them too rudely away from the familiar. For instance, the stripped classicism of Paul Cret (1876–1945) and others was popular for institutional architecture in the thirties and even later, but its reduction of columns to square piers, even to flutings in heavy wall surfaces, its academic compositional scheme that often lacked the boldness and contrast of true classicism, were not really satisfactory unless handled with great sensitivity (Fig. 147).

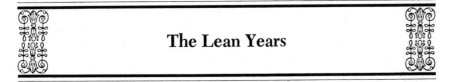

The Lean Years

Historical forces probably had as much to do with the decline of Eclecticism as anything else. The great waves of immigration from Italy and elsewhere were long over, and the craftsmen who executed the detailing of an Eclectic building were increasingly likely to be second-generation Americans who had chosen to be stone carvers, bronzefounders, terra-cotta modelers, or mosaicists in spite of a broadening range of occupations open to them. There may, then, have been fewer such artisans available by the end of the 1920s than twenty years before, and probably at much higher wages. The Depression, of course, severely curtailed all building, whatever the cost, and perhaps, the government aside, only the film industry, source of cheap escape that it was, could afford to build lavishly; the movie house was often Modernistic. Architects were turned out to pasture, measuring buildings for the Historic American Buildings Survey or sitting in their offices, thinking of what they might do some day.

Eclectic architecture was still produced in the thirties and during the Second World War, but the heart seems to have gone out of it. Without the large budgets of the previous years, with many of the great Eclectic architects and their supporting artists and craftsmen dead or retired, the buildings executed too often lacked something in their proportions, detailing, and materials that might have brought them to life. The failure may have been more one of artistry than of anything else. A good architect can build very simply if he must, relying on proportion and a few simple moldings—the Greek Revival shows this time and again. But after 1930, there was too much of a feeling that a cheap-looking pediment or pointed arch was better than none at all and this, combined with a somehow blunted sense of scale, proportion, and relief, produced many a negligible suburban church, many a frail yet stuffy-looking builder's house. The attempts to compromise with new demands by including features from "modern" architecture—big windows, informal massings—usually made matters all the worse.

Another aspect of the loss of heart was, very probably, a weakening sense of the significance of a certain style for a certain building type. Naturally, a great many clients had always commissioned a Gothic or a Colonial church, a Colonial or Tudor house, because anything else would be unseemly. But this attitude seems more and more to have approached an ossified universality in the thirties, at the same time that the most talented new architects increasingly became modernists by education and conviction. A figure to be encountered in the 1940s, and even later, was the Embittered Old Classicist (or Gothicist), sometimes a sensitive artist society no longer wanted or could no longer afford, more often an honest tradesman whose wares were no longer in demand.

Survivals

And yet Eclecticism is not dead, even though it may be logy (Fig. 148).[135] Period interiors, sometimes incorporating genuinely antique furniture and genuinely antique paneling, are still being installed. Period buildings, such as the recent branches of the Franklin National Bank in New York, the Frick Art Building at the University of Pittsburgh, and Palladian villas at Palm Beach, are still being erected that are only slightly meager by the standards of 1920. Good reproduction furniture is still made, for a price. The current fashion for heavy restoration, even reproduction *ex nihilo*, of historic buildings is evidence of an Eclectic spirit, one content with the illusion in lieu of the reality (Fig. 149). Colonial Williamsburg, Inc. licenses reproduction glass, wallpaper, and for that matter flatware (Fig. 150). Highly priced decorator magazines, such as *Architectural Digest*, attest to the continuing vogue of period decoration. On a lower level, the Sunday real-estate pages of any newspaper offer new, if degenerate, Eclectic architecture for sale.

Even a sort of Eclectic ideology has flared up recently. In *The Golden City* (Doubleday, 1959), Henry Hope Reed exhibited contrasting details from "American Renaissance" and "secessionist" (i.e., "modern") architecture and offered a dissenting theory of the history of architecture since the mid-nineteenth century. Since then, Reed and others have prophesied the triumphant return of classicism to American architecture, and in the last few years a group associated with Reed has formed Classical America, an association, which publishes a well-designed occasional magazine of the same name (Figs. 151, 152).[136]

Thus, Eclecticism is not to be regarded as a totally closed episode. If enough people, particularly intelligent, eloquent ones, regard it as worth reviving, it doubtless will be renewed in some form or other. Robert Venturi has written favorably of the compositions of an Italian Eclectic, Armando Brazini, and in his recent *Learning from Las Vegas* (M.I.T., 1972) he points out the symbolic significance for Middle America of such Eclectic devices as the window shutter.[137] Out of such remarks, a new and revitalized Eclecticism may some day come into being; indeed, perhaps only a cogent theory in support of it is needed to allow its continuing existence to be legitimized.

Epilogue

Eclecticism today is like a person who has almost lived down an ancient scandal, a person whose crime was once exposed, but who is now regarded merely as old and harmless, if not quite respectable. Thirty or forty years ago, the prevailing critical indictment of Eclecticism went somewhat this way: *Eclecticism is the artistically valueless imitation of old, and therefore irrelevant, architectural styles for the gratification of the predatory, philistine rich by sentimental or dishonest architects who ignore their duty to create a vital twentieth-century architecture at the service of the people*— a judgment combining aesthetic evaluation, character analysis, and social commentary. More recently, the indictment has been repeated less often and less vehemently, though it remains in the docket, and even a measure of appreciation has reappeared. Individual Eclectic buildings have been the subjects of recent preservation efforts, if only to prevent something worse from replacing them, and there has been a certain mild attention to their artistic qualities and their craftsmanship.

And yet, the stylistic imitation remains a mark of Cain. Since the beginning of the Romantic period, originality, rather than taste, usually has been regarded as the most necessary condition for true art; the Eclectic's willful resignation of originality has seemed therefore like an admission that instead of practicing architecture as an art, he was engaging in the sort of para-scholarly exercise that goes into the making of film sets.[138]

It does not help matters that we are out of sympathy with the architect's rich clients, who so often commissioned the mansions, the factories and office buildings, and sat on the boards and committees that ordered the museums, the libraries, and the clubhouses. We think of these wealthy people as selfish and pretentious, conceited and foolish, and their patronage seems to damn doubly the Eclectic architecture they commissioned, regarding it as suitable to their self-image and life style. Nor are we in much greater sympathy with the middle classes of the teens and twenties. Only a few years ago, the Come to Church posters still advertised the act of worship in a way that would have seemed normal in 1925:

smiling, eugenic Caucasians—the same that once populated department-store advertisements: the husband hatted and overcoated, the wife and daughter dressed in their best clothes, hats and white gloves included—walk toward the little Colonial church on the knoll. A good thing for respectable people to do, but even for the believers among us, the image is increasingly one of a stuffy and bourgeois ritual, with Homburg and Georgian steeple among its implements.[139]

A new look at Eclecticism, one with an openness to the pleasure that it might offer us today, will probably depend as much on our understanding the Eclectic architect and his client as human beings as it does on our readiness to consider the artistic merits of a revived architecture or our willing suspension of disbelief regarding certain arches and beams. Eclecticism is one of those phases in architectural history when the human factor was involved most conspicuously, one whose works are beyond a certain point incomprehensible without understanding and lending sympathy to an earlier generation, its society, and its attitudes. If we can establish that the Eclectic architect and his client were not two-dimensional monsters, and that Eclectic architecture was at its best a carefully considered, fully appreciated response to the cultural values architect and client shared, then we can be less inhibited about investigating what the forms, colors, and textures of Eclectic architecture have to offer us, seeing all things even with the eyes of our own time.

It is unlikely that the cultured individual will ever find this Eclecticism completely satisfactory again. It departed too far, too often, from the basic problems of shelter and construction and their most natural solutions. Its historic ornamentation too often smells of the lamp. Its allegories in sculpture and fresco communicated too little to the public even when new. And—unlike Eclecticism, say, in Scandinavia—it took itself a little too seriously. But the care in the design and craftsmanship in the execution of Eclectic architecture nonetheless created possibilities for visual experience that go beyond fashion and are still valid.

1. Interior of house, Cleveland, built 1926.

2. Isaiah Temple, Chicago, ca. 1924. Alfred S. Alschuler. A Byzantine-Moorish design, in allusion to the Near Eastern origins of Judaism.

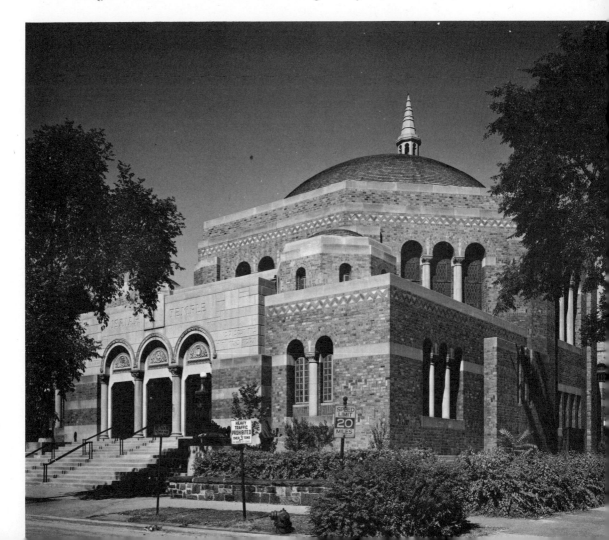

3. Cleveland Museum of Art, Cleveland, 1916. Hubbell and Benes. The art museum as a municipal jewel box, set in a Beaux-Arts entourage of shrubs and trees.

4. Pittsburgh Athletic Association, Pittsburgh, 1909–11. Janssen and Abbott. A palatial clubhouse in Venetian Renaissance, in Pittsburgh's Civic Center.

5. The Parthenon, Nashville, originally built 1896, rebuilt 1920s. W. C. Smith, after Ictinus and Callicrates; George J. Zolnay, sculptor, after Phidias. Erected in lath and plaster for the Tennessee Centennial Exposition, this full-size replica was later rebuilt in concrete.

6. City Hall, Stockholm, 1908–23. Ragnar Östberg. Eclecticism was also prevalent in Europe in the late nineteenth and early twentieth centuries; this subtle and sumptuous example of Nordic "national romanticism" was much admired by American Eclectics, though not imitated.

Design Patented April 25th 1871.

The above cut represents a

Design Patented by C. Graham & Son,

ARCHITECTS OF ELIZABETH, N. J.,

which may be applied to French roofs of any size or description, forming a great and acknowledged improvement in the ornamentation of French roofs—destroying the monotony of continuous slating, and presenting to the eye a beautiful, bold, and characteristic feature—particularly adapted for fronts of smaller cottages, as represented in cut.

DESIGNS FURNISHED

embodying said Patent in various designs. Also plans, specifications and working drawings for the same. Also the right to use said Patent designs on application to

C. GRAHAM & SON,

ARCHITECTS,

ELIZABETH, N. J.

7. Advertisement for a set of slate patterning designs, 1871. C. Graham and Son. This brittle wooden house, with its high, patterned mansard roof, represents everything the Eclectics despised.

8. Sketch for cabinetwork, 1876. William G. Preston. American Eastlake, showing the influence of Talbert's architectonic designs.

9. Queen Anne city house, 1879. J. A. and W. J. Wilson. To be built of red brick and red terra-cotta; the combination of single- and multi-paned window sashes was common; it was intended to allow a clear view out while imparting a certain quaintness to the facade.

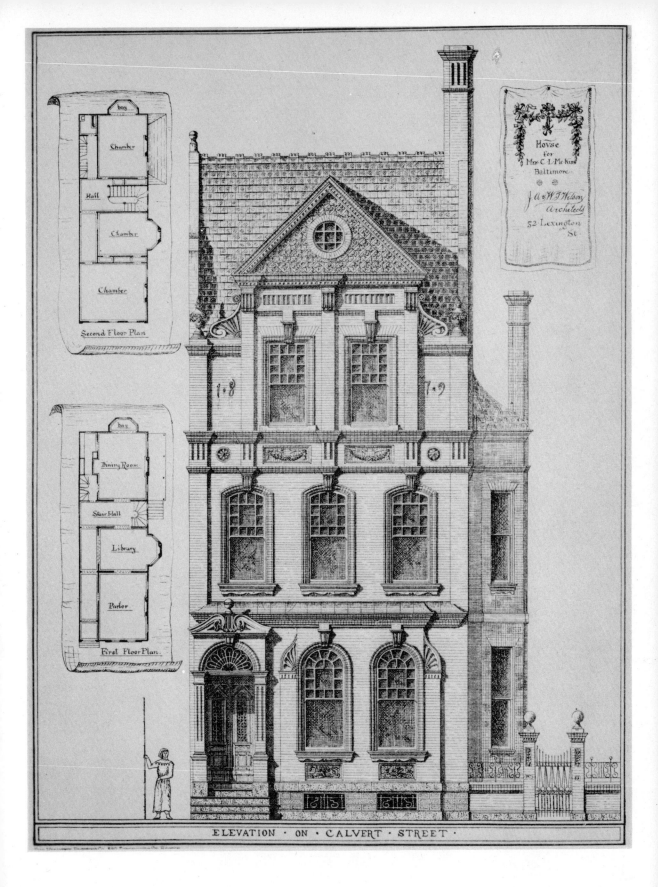

Second Floor Plan

Chamber

Hall

Chamber

Chamber

bay

First Floor Plan.

Dining Room

Stair Hall

Library

Parlor

bay

Hovse
for
Mrs C. L. McKim
Baltimore

J & W T Wilson
Architects
52 Lexington
St

ELEVATION · ON · CALVERT · STREET ·

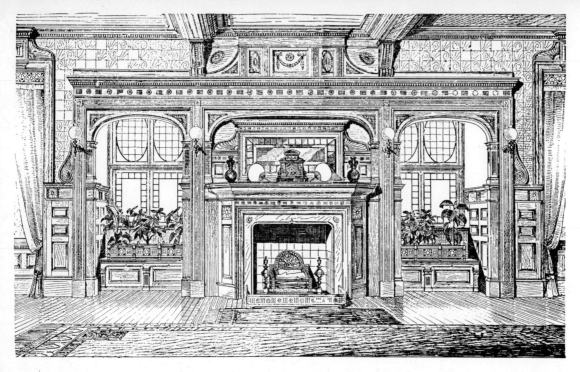

10. Queen Anne interior, 1880. Potter and Robertson. A mixture of styles—vaguely Georgian, a little Jacobean, and some Japanese touches.

11. Shavian Manorial house, 1879. W. A. Bates. A typical Shavian Manorial layering of materials, story by story, under an artfully composed set of roofs.

House at Orange, N.J.
Edw. T. Hapgood,
Archt.

from "Building"

12. Early Colonial Revival house, late 1880s. Edward T. Hapgood. Formality and informality—notably in the symmetrical hipped roof that is caught up in an Aesthetic game of roof planes as it descends—are mixed charmingly in this shingled house.

13. Early Shingle Style house, 1879. William Ralph Emerson. During the 1870s the roof was often the most important element in the design of a house, its planes cut, folded, and stretched to cover the irregular perimeter of the walls.

HOUSE for T. R. Glover Esq.
MILTON. Wm. R. Emerson; Archt.

HOUSE at DELANO PARK:
Shore of Cape Elizabeth.

14. Shingle Style house, 1885. Stevens and Cobb. Native rubble laid up
to suggest dry-wall construction, shingles weathered gray, roof stained
moss green, and white trim.

15. Living hall, ca. 1885. Stevens and Cobb. The living hall, a habitable
circulation space, was fashionable in suburban and seaside houses in the
eighties.

Main Staircase.

16. *Envoi* of a Rotch Traveling Scholar: Hôtel de Cluny, Paris, 1889.
Rendering by Henry Bacon, Jr. Such *envois* served partly as student
exercises, partly as reference material for others; this one is by the future
architect of the Lincoln Memorial.

17. A parlor in Brooklyn Heights, New York, ca. 1890.

18. Imaginary scene by Henry P. Kirby, ca. 1890. Kirby's *Architectural Compositions* (1892) was filled with medieval fantasies of this sort.

19. Trinity Church, Boston, 1873–78; central tower probably designed 1874; western towers rebuilt in 1890s. Henry Hobson Richardson, with Stanford White; John LaFarge, decorator. The church in the late seventies, with the original western towers; to the right, rear, the Brattle Square Church.

20. Allegheny County Courthouse, Pittsburgh, 1884–88. Henry Hobson Richardson. Though the jail gains most of the attention today, the Courthouse can boast the finest of Richardson's towers.

21. Allegheny County Courthouse: entrance detail. Richardson's handling of ornament and materials was much admired by the Eclectics.

22. William K. Vanderbilt house, New York, 1879. Richard Morris Hunt. Demolished. To the boxy, brownstone, remotely Italianate houses of mid-Victorian New York the Vanderbilt house opposed individualism, limestone, and scholarship.

23. "The Breakers," Newport, 1892–95: great hall. Richard Morris Hunt. An interior for the Vanderbilts: Caen stone, accented with variegated marble and bronze.

24. Wisconsin state capitol, Madison, 1907–17. George B. Post and Sons; Karl Bitter, sculptor. A unique cruciform plan allows entrance porches directly beneath the St. Paul's-type dome, with Bitter's allegorical groups as transitional features.

25. American Surety Building, New York, 1895. Bruce Price. An early palazzo skyscraper in New York; to the left, Upjohn's Trinity Church of 1839–46, which the Eclectics respected.

26.   Germantown Cricket Club, Philadelphia, 1890; wings 1902. McKim, Mead and White. A fine piece of Colonial Revival; its spare style and the feeling it shows for Philadelphia Colonial suggest the hand of McKim, who spent his boyhood in Germantown.

27.   Boston Public Library, Boston, 1888–98. McKim, Mead and White; Charles Follen McKim, designer. Suggested by Labrouste's Bibliothèque Ste-Geneviève in Paris and Alberti's Tempio Malatestiano at Rimini.

28. Low Library, Columbia University, New York, begun ca. 1895. McKim, Mead and White; Charles Follen McKim, designer. General conception Imperial Roman, most details Greek, cheneau Beaux-Arts, window sash America 1895; in the background, Allen and Collens' Riverside Church of 1927–30.

29. Morgan Library, New York, 1906. McKim, Mead and White; Charles Follen McKim, designer; H. Siddons Mowbray, muralist. The sumptuous library annex of Morgan's house.

30. Watts Sherman house, Newport: library, ca. 1880. Stanford White. An apple-green-and-gold interior in Richardson's Shavian Manorial house of 1874.

31.   House for the Tiffany family, New York, 1884. Stanford White and
Louis Comfort Tiffany, designers. Demolished. Above the Richardsonian
basement, the walls are of golden-brown "Tiffany brick," a variety of
the "Roman brick" White had introduced two years before.

32.   C. A. Whittier house (right) by McKim, Mead and White; H. L.
Higginson house (left) by Henry Hobson Richardson; Boston, 1881.
Both demolished. Richardson and the designer of the Whittier house,
probably White, intended their works to harmonize.

33. Villard houses, New York, ca. 1884. McKim, Mead and White; Joseph Morrill Wells, designer of façades; Stanford White, John Lafarge, and Augustus Saint-Gaudens, decorators of Villard's residence. This palatial complex was executed in brownstone at Villard's insistence rather than the limestone that Wells intended.

34.   Madison Square Garden, New York, 1889. McKim, Mead and White;
Stanford White, designer. Demolished. Part north Italian, part Spanish, in
white terra-cotta and pale buff brick; on top of the Giralda-like tower, the
second version of Saint-Gaudens' *Diana*.

35. New York Herald Building, New York, 1894. McKim, Mead and White; Stanford White, designer. Demolished. Fra Giocondo's Palazzo del Consiglio at Verona inspired the detailing for this long-gone newspaper plant, presses below, offices above, in marble and cream terra-cotta.

36. Memorial Arch, Washington Square, New York, 1892. McKim, Mead and White; Stanford White, designer; Alexander Milne Calder and Frederick MacMonnies, sculptors. Erected to celebrate the centenary of Washington's inaugural, in place of the original, temporary arch of 1889; in the background, the campanile of White's Judson Memorial Church (1892).

37. Madison Square Presbyterian Church, New York, 1906. McKim, Mead and White; Stanford White, designer; Adolph Weinman, sculptor. Demolished. Probably the first important American building to use polychrome terra cotta, which was set with deliberate unevenness.

38. A student's solution to a problem posed to a third-year class at M.I.T. in 1890: "An arched entrance with balcony above, designed for a public building." Edgar V. Seeler, designer and renderer. This was the winning design—the best of an indifferent lot, to judge by the jury's remarks—in a monthly competition.

39. Appellate Division, New York State Supreme Court, New York, 1900: courtroom. James Brown Lord; Edwin Howland Blashfield, painter. This over-rich, slightly awkward decor is typical of many grand interiors at the end of the nineteenth century.

40. *World's Columbian Exposition, Chicago, 1893: Court of Honor. Demolished. The center of the White City, with the cornice level at sixty feet.*

41. World's Columbian Exposition: Administration Building. Richard Morris Hunt. Demolished. Beaux-Arts in style, like much else at the fair, this building had an outer black-and-gold dome 275 feet high and a top-lighted rotunda inside 190 feet high.

42. World's Columbian Exposition: New York State Building. McKim, Mead and White. Demolished. Inspired partly by the Villa Medici, home of the Prix de Rome winners, this building has the slightly pompous gaiety found in much public architecture of the nineties.

43.   Metropolitan Museum of Art, New York: Fifth Avenue entrance, begun ca. 1895. Richard Morris Hunt and Richard Howland Hunt; Karl Bitter, sculptor. The present main entrance, a Beaux-Arts composition with unorthodox but beautiful capitals; the rough masonry above the ressauts was never carved into trophies as intended.

44.   "Biltmore," the Vanderbilt estate near Asheville, 1895. Richard Morris Hunt.

CASCADES FR.N.W.   E. BOEHL PH.

45. Louisiana Purchase Exposition, St. Louis, 1904: Festival Hall. Cass Gilbert. Demolished. Possibly the most extravagant Beaux-Arts work ever built in the U.S., with a wood and staff dome—claimed to be wider than that of St. Peter's.

46. Beaux-Arts houses in New York by Flagg and Chambers, 1899 (left), and Carrere and Hastings, 1896. The "American basement" plan had by the nineties replaced the old-fashioned high stoop in New York; reception and service areas were at ground level, social rooms on the floor above.

47. House of Senator William A. Clark, New York, 1903. Lord, Hewlett and Hull: Kenneth M. Murchison; H. Deglane. Demolished. A parvenu house, never much admired and here shown under demolition in 1927.

48. The Ansonia, New York, ca. 1900. W. E. D. Stokes, with Graves and Duboy. A Parisian apartment house blown up to fantastic dimensions, creating equally fantastic demands for stonecutting, ironwork, and skilled bricklaying.

49. The Ansonia: lobby. The interior as it was around 1918, judging from the service flag; the middle distance of the outer world for many people.

50. Singer Building, New York, 1908 (left center). Ernest Flagg. Demolished. A Beaux-Arts skyscraper, here shown in a pre-1916 thicket of tall buildings.

←─ SINGER BDG.

SINGER BLDG. & BROADWAY NORTH. C-9772
Copyright 1909 By
IRVING UNDERHILL, New York.

51. Grand Central Terminal, New York, 1903–13. Reed and Stem, then Warren and Wetmore, architects; Jules Coutan, sculptor. A grand civic ornament, in the spirit of the once-popular concept of the railroad station as the gateway to a city.

52. Union Station, Pittsburgh, 1900. D. H. Burnham and Co. The station is preceded by a fantastic cab shelter, so huge that buses have passed through its smaller arches.

53. New York Public Library, New York, 1898–1911. Carrere and Hastings. An elaborate but slightly crowded Beaux-Arts composition in marble forms the entrance; in the background, center, the American Radiator Building (1924) by Raymond Hood.

54. Allegheny County Soldiers' and Sailors' Memorial, Pittsburgh, 1907. Palmer and Hornbostel. The Halicarnassus theme used for a tall auditorium building with an ambulatory full of flags and uniforms.

55. Pennsylvania Station, New York, 1906–10: concourse. McKim, Mead and White; Charles Follen McKim, designer. Demolished. Modeled after the tepidarium of the Baths of Caracalla, the concourse was 300 feet long and nearly 150 feet high; above walls in which travertine received perhaps its American debut were pastel maps of the Pennsylvania system by Jules Guerin.

56. New York Stock Exchange, New York, 1901–4. George B. Post and Sons; J. Q. A. Ward and Paul Bartlett, sculptors. The grandest of all temples of finance, with *Integrity Protecting the Works of Man* in the pediment.

57. John Wanamaker department store, Philadelphia, 1902–10. D. H. Burnham and Co. A commercial palazzo taking up half a Philadelphia "square"; to the right, City Hall.

58. New (or Century) Theatre, New York, opened 1909. Carrere and Hastings. Demolished. Shown here under construction, with keystones, window surrounds, and portions of the frieze blocked out for carving *in situ* that seems never to have been executed.

59. University Club, New York, 1900. McKim, Mead and White; Charles Follen McKim, designer. A study in subtle variations of relief and texture, heightened with carving and ironwork.

60. University Club, New York: entrance. McKim was generally cool to French architecture, but this entrance is adapted from one in the Louvre.

61.   The Apthorp, New York, 1908. Clinton and Russell. A neighbor of the Ansonia, and only a few years later, the Apthorp shows the turn away from Beaux-Arts extravagances in the late 1900s.

62.   New York Municipal Building, 1911–14. McKim, Mead and White: Edward Kendall, designer; Adolph Weinman, sculptor. The typical "capital" of a pre-1916 skyscraper surmounted by a tower inspired by Renaissance cathedral architecture.

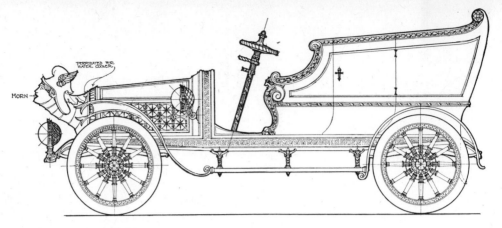

63. An Eclectic automobile, 1906. William L. Welton, designer. The head is that of Mercury, god of traffic.

64. Hudson River Day Line steamer *Washington Irving*, 1913. Destroyed. Frank H. Kirby and J. W. Millard and Brother, naval architects. Four hundred fourteen feet long, eighty-six feet over guards, six thousand passengers; the forward funnel is a dummy.

65. The *Washington Irving*: Alhambra writing room. Louis O. Keil, designer. The *Irving* was decorated to suggest the settings of its namesake's books.

66. Queensboro Bridge, New York, 1909: finial. Gustav Lindenthal, engineer; Henry Hornbostel, architect. Dismayed by Lindenthal's raw-boned bridge, cautiously overdesigned to make early use of nickel steel, Hornbostel tried to add a few gracious touches such as this riveter's version of a rostral column.

67. *Fame*: pendentive fresco from the Hudson County Courthouse. Jersey City, ca. 1910. Edwin Howland Blashfield, painter. A typical allegorical painting by one of the most famous muralists of the pre-1915 period.

68. Mercury group from Grand Central Terminal, New York, ca. 1913. Jules Coutan, sculptor. Mercury is accompanied by Hercules, Minerva, and the American Eagle.

69. Murray's Roman Gardens, New York, ca. 1908: dining room. Erkins Studios, decorator. Demolished. An improbable remodeling of an old schoolhouse into a Times Square night spot; a mirror wall doubles the apparent size.

70. Page from a guide for draftsmen, 1914. Such guides gently pushed the product and offered practical advice on detailing it.

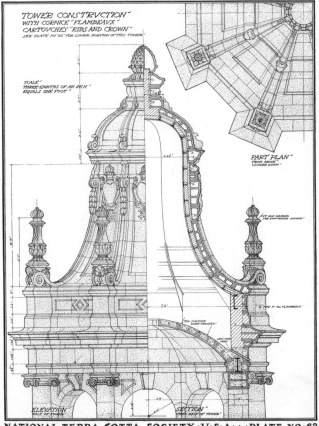

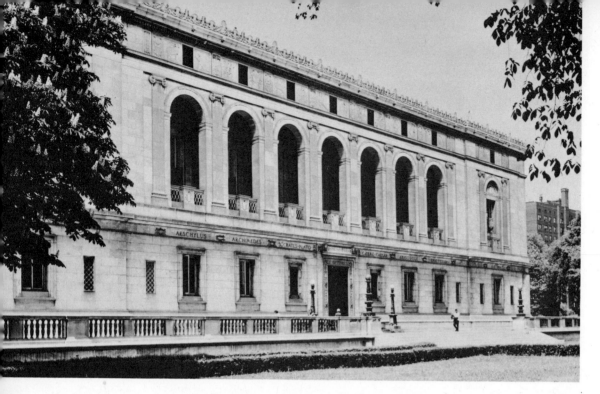

71.   Detroit Public Library, Detroit, 1921. Cass Gilbert. A McKim, Mead and White "alumnus" reflects here the design of the Boston Public Library in the quieter taste of three decades later.

72.   Henry C. Frick house (now Frick Collection), New York. Carrere and Hastings, 1914; remodeled as a museum by John Russell Pope, 1935. A town mansion for an industrialist, whose fabulous wealth is attested both by his art collection, selected by Duveen, and the ample lawn space on Fifth Avenue.

73. City Hall, San Francisco, 1912–15. Bakewell and Brown; Arthur Brown, Jr., designer. The dome of St. Peter's has been adapted and placed on an official building treated according to a standard formula of the period.

74. Scribner Building, New York, 1913. Ernest Flagg. Flagg's characteristic contrast of large- and small-scale elements is well shown in this building, a bookstore with publisher's offices above.

75. Carnegie Institute of Technology, Pittsburgh; entrance corridor; College of Fine Arts, 1912–16. Henry Hornbostel; J. M. Hewlett, artist. Hornbostel, who directed Carnegie Tech's architectural program, worked out an elaborate didactic program of decorations for the College of Fine Arts.

76. Free Library of Philadelphia, 1927. Horace Trumbauer. This and a sister building alongside are major elements of Philadelphia's City Beautiful gesture, the Parkway; their style is imitated from Gabriel's buildings on the Place de la Concorde.

77. Panama-Pacific Exposition, San Francisco, 1915: Court of Flowers. George W. Kelham. Demolished. Travertine color, with pink walls and accents of golden yellow and red; in the foreground, Solon Borglum's *American Pioneer*; in the court itself, Edgar Walter's *Beauty and the Beast*.

78. Panama-Pacific Exposition: Palace of Fine Arts. Bernard Maybeck. Rebuilt in concrete, ca. 1968. With inspiration from Boecklin's *Isle of the Dead* and Gérome's *Chariot Race*, Maybeck created a romantically classical complex intended to induce a feeling of "modified melancholy."

79. H. A. C. Taylor house, Newport, 1885. McKim, Mead and White. Demolished. Perhaps the first Colonial Revival house in which symmetry —not quite perfect yet—is observed.

80. Clarence Mackay house, Roslyn, L.I., 1906. McKim, Mead and White; Stanford White, designer. Demolished. The exterior of the Mackay house recalled a Louis XIII chateau; imposing though not ostentatious, this hall, with its exuberant stair in the style of Grinling Gibbons, is Carolean.

81. "Bonniecrest," Newport, 1912–18: hallway. John Russell Pope. An archaeological but homey Tudor house by an architect best known for his cool, even chilly, classicism.

82. Garden of "Villa Vizcaya," Miami, ca. 1916. Diego Suarez, landscape architect. An Italian garden, conceived in a Rococo spirit, for one of the greatest Florida mansions.

83. Percy Pyne house, New York, 1911. McKim, Mead and White. An Early Federal townhouse formula, elaborated to give the third floor a prominence equal to that of the second.

84. Russell Alger house, Grosse Pointe, 1910. Charles A. Platt. The concentration of a few pieces of refined ornament at focal points on an otherwise plain façade is typical of Platt's work.

85. "Gwinn," Bratenahl, Ohio, 1906: library. Charles A. Platt. A paneled interior in an Italianate villa on the shores of Lake Erie.

86. House, ca. 1910. This unidentified house is typical of many in its free use of motifs from sources only to be guessed at—in this case the Prairie School plus the Greek Revival, perhaps.

87. Highland Towers Apartments, 1913. Frederick Scheibler. Wrightian influence, or possibly the Viennese Secession, may have inspired this composition in warm light-brown brick with panels of dark blue tile in cream-colored plaster.

88. Illustration from *The Frozen Fountain* (1932). Claude Bragdon, designer and renderer. Apparently a suggestion for furnishing a typical New York apartment; the cabinet is decorated with a tracing of a "knight's move" magic square.

89. Panama-Pacific Exposition: Court of the Ages (or of Abundance). Louis Christian Mullgardt. Demolished. In the tower archway, *The Rise of Civilization*, by Chester Beach; in the center, the Fountain of the Earth, by Robert Aitken; to the right, the dome of the Palace of Mines, by Bliss and Faville.

90. Opposite, Cunard Building, New York, 1921. Benjamin Wistar Morris. A classical tall building of the post-1921 period; the usual embarrassment caused by setbacks is alleviated by the location on Bowling Green.

91. Church of the Ascension, Pittsburgh, 1897. William Halsey Wood. Halsey Wood, like Cram, had ambitions to reform the architecture of the Episcopal Church; here, he has produced a handsome but fairly typical piece of 1890s Gothic.

92. Cathedral Church of St. John the Divine, New York: choir, begun after 1892 by Heins and LaFarge; nave begun 1911 and choir vaulting and clerestory rebuilt by Cram, Goodhue and Ferguson. LaFarge's abortive choir and Cram's "hall-church" nave are separated by the cyclopean Victorian engineering of the crossing, whose completion remains a challenge.

93. East Liberty Presbyterian Church, Pittsburgh, 1931–35. Cram and Ferguson; John Angel, sculptor. The Presbyterian chancel that was never converted to Catholicism; the high relief represents the Last Supper.

94. Church of the New Jerusalem (Swedenborgian Cathedral), Bryn Athyn, Pa., begun 1913. Cram and Ferguson, architects of the church. Here, before disputes led to his resignation, Cram experimented to excess with medieval design refinements, then the subject of much scholarly interest, and with the use of resident craftsmen to execute sculpture, glass, stonecutting, metalwork, and joinery.

95. Chapel of St. George's School, Newport, 1924–28: cloister. Cram and Ferguson. Early Perpendicular like the rest of the chapel, the cloister seems to owe most to the late fourteenth-century cloister of Gloucester Cathedral, though the heavy transverse arches create a different effect from the rippling movement of the original.

96. Lovett Hall, Rice Institute (now Rice University), Houston, 1912. Cram, Goodhue and Ferguson; Ralph Adams Cram, designer. In his autobiography Cram tries to explain why he chose a hybrid Mediterranean style for a college building in Texas.

97. St. Thomas' Church, New York, 1911: chancel, showing the reredos of 1918. Cram, Goodhue and Ferguson; Bertram Grosvenor Goodhue, designer; Lee Lawrie, sculptor. This soaring reredos, pierced by three windows of deep blue glass flecked with red, won Goodhue the Gold Medal of the A.I.A.

98. Church of St. Vincent Ferrer, New York, 1915. Bertram Grosvenor Goodhue; Lee Lawrie, sculptor. One of Goodhue's finest Gothic façades, showing his brilliant weaving of vertical and horizontal elements.

99. St. Bartholomew's, New York, 1918. Bertram Grosvenor Goodhue. A sumptuous church on the new Park Avenue made possible by the electrification of the Grand Central tracks; the free Romanesque style was determined by the retention of Stanford White's portico, survivor of an earlier St. Bartholomew's.

100. Panama-California Exposition, San Diego, 1916: California Building. Bertram Grosvenor Goodhue. Another celebration of the Canal, the San Diego fair was resolutely Spanish; its key building was this Churrigueresque Mexican essay by Goodhue, still standing.

101. State Capitol, Lincoln, begun 1922. Bertram Grosvenor Goodhue; Lee Lawrie, sculptor. Here, Goodhue simplifies classicism in a way influential in official architecture for the next fifteen years; a token dome, atop a tall office tower, supports Lawrie's *Sower*.

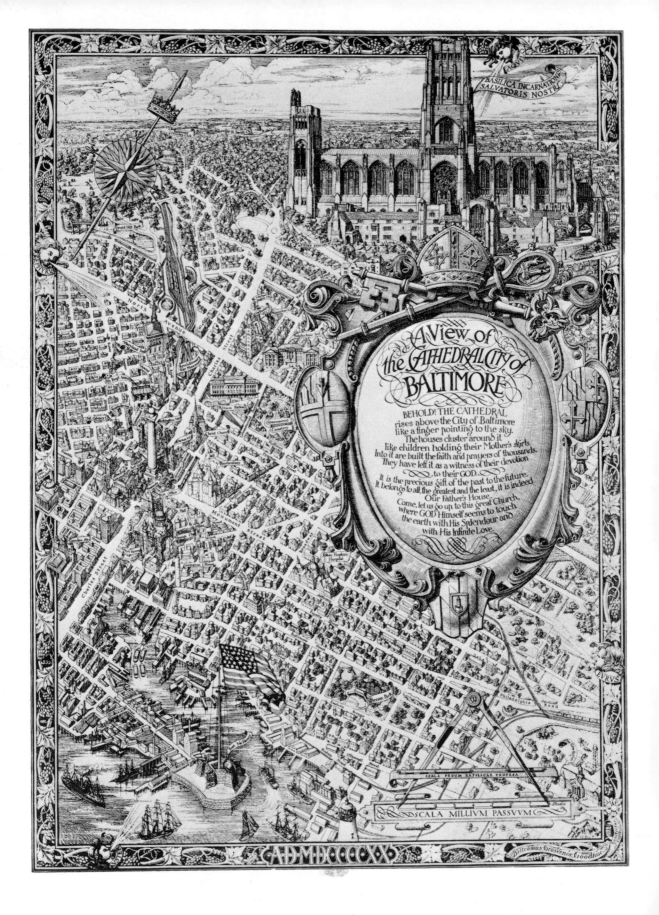

BASILICA INCARNATIONIS SALVATORIS NOSTRI

A View of the CATHEDRAL CITY of BALTIMORE

BEHOLD! THE CATHEDRAL
rises above the City of Baltimore
like a finger pointing to the sky.
The houses cluster around it
like children holding their Mother's skirts.
Into it are built the faith and prayers of thousands.
They have left it as a witness of their devotion
to their GOD.
It is the precious gift of the past to the future.
It belongs to all, the greatest and the least, it is indeed
Our Father's House.
Come, let us go up to this great Church,
where GOD Himself seems to touch
the earth with His Splendour and
with His Infinite Love.

SCALA PEDUM BASILICAE PROPRIA

SCALA MILLIVM PASSVVM

A·D·MDCCCCXX

Bertramus Grosvenor Goodhue

102. Presentation drawing of a design for the Cathedral of Maryland (Episcopal), 1920. Bertram Grosvenor Goodhue, architect and renderer. A Goodhue fantasy, in the form of a seventeenth-century perspective map, with the size of the proposed cathedral greatly exaggerated.

103. Harkness Memorial complex, Yale, ca. 1918. James Gamble Rogers. There must be steelwork in the tower, and some of the steps were ground down to make them look old, but this remains nevertheless a very seductive design.

104. Memorial Tower, University of Pennsylvania, Philadelphia, 1901. Cope and Stewardson. A rather unrestrained Jacobean, used with a good deal of verve by a Philadelphia office that specialized in institutional architecture.

105. Cathedral of Learning, University of Pittsburgh, begun 1928. Charles Z. Klauder. One of the supreme architectural conceits of the 1920s.

106. Woolworth Building, New York, completed 1913. Cass Gilbert. Once the tallest office building in the world, this terra-cotta essay in Flemish Gothic anticipated the post-1916 skyscraper in its insistent verticality and its prominent use of setbacks.

107. Union Trust Company, Pittsburgh, 1915. F. J. Österling; designer probably Pierre A. Liesch. In the spirit of the Woolworth Building, Flemish Gothic, executed in terra cotta.

108. Chicago Tribune Building, begun 1922. Hood and Howells. The prize-winning design in the international competition of 1922, it was soon to be regarded as a classic example of bad architecture.

109. Willard Straight house, New York, 1914. Delano and Aldrich who were among the foremost designers of white-on-red Neo-Georgian houses, clubs, and churches; a town mansion such as this had counterparts hardly less formal in the suburbs.

110. Newbold Farm, Laverock, Pa., ca. 1920. Mellor, Meigs and Howe. A group of buildings for a gentleman farmer in the Norman Farmhouse style, with contrasted forms and textures, in a low-keyed range of color, used in place of ornament.

111. Neil-Mauran double house, Philadelphia, 1890. Wilson Eyre. A red brick house, with a little delicate carving, Quattrocento in feeling, in brownstone over the doorways.

112. "Low Walls," Rosemont, Pa., 1908. Wilson Eyre. One of Eyre's English-inspired suburban houses, relying on contrasting shapes and materials rather than ornament.

113. University Museum, Philadelphia, begun 1893. Wilson Eyre; Frank Miles Day and Brother; Cope and Stewardson. The museum's Lombardic style, expressed in dark red brick with very thick joints, was established by Eyre; inside one particularly nice detail is the marble tablets on which the allowable floor loads are elegantly lettered.

114. Borie Bank, Philadelphia, 1896. Wilson Eyre. A not-too-serious essay in Georgian from several periods; the balconies are copied from one on Congress Hall, a few blocks away.

115. Office of Mellor, Meigs and Howe, Philadelphia, 1912: the "big room." The fashionable Eclectics met their clients in rooms like this one.

116. Semi-detached houses, Chestnut Hill, Philadelphia, 1913. Edmund B. Gilchrist. Built for a real-estate organization that developed much of Chestnut Hill, these houses, more English than anything else, represent an attempt to supply moderately priced housing of high quality.

117. "French village," Mount Airy, Philadelphia: gate lodge, 1925. Robert Rodes McGoodwin. A development of high-priced houses built of a local silvery-gray schist laid in well-buttered joints of warm-tinted mortar.

118. "High Hollow," Chestnut Hill, Philadelphia, 1913–14. Mellor, Meigs and Howe; George Howe, designer. The architect's own house; fifteen years later, as a partner of William Lescaze, he was designing houses in the International Style.

119. Craig Heberton house, Montecito, California, 1916. George Washington Smith. Smith, a stockbroker turned architect, relied on picturesque massing and fenestration rather than ornament in his Spanish Colonial Revival work.

120. Santa Barbara County Courthouse, Santa Barbara, 1929. William Mooser and Company. A somewhat undisciplined interpretation of Spanish Colonial Revival.

121. Everglades Club, Palm Beach, 1918. Addison Mizner. An early example of the imaginative stylistic melanges that Mizner, improvising at great expense, was to create for the wealthy of Florida during the boom years.

122. Zimmerman house, Albuquerque, 1929. W. Miles Brittelle. The need of the Pueblo Style to compromise with the modern demand for large windows has produced a house that, aside from the authentic-looking *vigas,* suggests a somewhat softened Irving Gill.

123. *St. George* and two hood-mold stops, *Football* and *Baseball,* chapel of St. George's School, Newport, ca. 1928. Cram and Ferguson; Joseph A. Coletti, sculptor. Under the Eclectics the style of a building usually said something about its purpose and traditions; sculpture made the message more explicit.

124. Cartoon for the Victory Window, Christ Church, Glendale, O., 1920. Charles J. Connick, glass stainers. Under the indignant shepherding of Cram and Connick, the stained-glass window, often treated as if it were a painting around 1900, was brought back to medieval design principles.

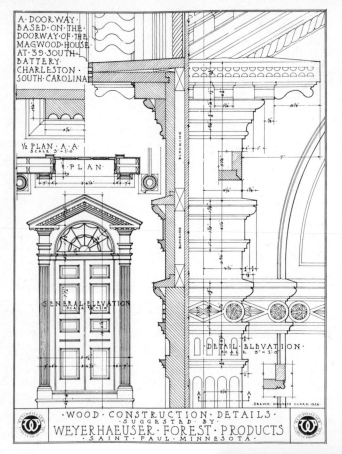

125. Drawing from the White Pine Series of Architectural Monographs, 1928. The White Pine Series was one of the scholarly (and gentlemanly) promotional publications to which the Eclectic was exposed; suitable for permanent binding, it came gratis to potential users of white pine.

126. Page from a catalogue of ready-made ornament, 1931. Executed in fibrous plaster, pressed wood, cement, and other easily shaped materials.

127. Federal Building, Cleveland, 1905. Brunner and Tryon. A typical official building for a large early twentieth-century city.

128. Supreme Court Building, Washington, 1935. Cass Gilbert. One of the last pieces of elaborate official classicism on a monumental scale.

129. Lincoln Memorial, Washington, finished 1922. Henry Bacon. Regarded as one of the most beautiful works of twentieth-century American architecture.

130. Jefferson Memorial, Washington, begun 1939. John Russell Pope. Pope's classicism is elegant but often rather bleak.

131. Minnesota State Capitol, St. Paul, 1896–1905. Cass Gilbert. A fairly typical capitol building of the Eclectic period, here with a dome modeled after that of St. Peter's.

132. United States Courthouse, New York, 1936. Cass Gilbert and Cass Gilbert, Jr. The official office building in its skyscraper variation.

133. U.S. Army Supply Base, Brooklyn, ca. 1918. Cass Gilbert. Gilbert's essay in near-functionalism was much applauded at the time.

134. H. E. Dodge house, Grosse Pointe, 1915. Albert Kahn. One of the very accomplished period designs of an office best remembered for its industrial architecture.

135. Shelton Hotel, New York, 1925: architect's rendering. Arthur Loomis Harmon. Admired for its powerful massing, the Shelton seemed to prove that the post-1916 skyscraper *could* be designed in a traditional style.

136. Jefferson Medical College, Philadelphia, 1928. Horace Trumbauer. A need for institutional dignity combined with a desire to express structural lightness and soaring verticals led to a use of the delicate Italian Romanesque style for multi-storied hospital and bank buildings in the twenties, despite the absence of a specific cultural context. Quattrocento, expecially the rusticated Florentine form, was also popular for such buildings.

137. Design for Chicago Tribune Building, 1922. Eliel Saarinen. This second-prize design was very influential in skyscraper design of the 1920s and early '30s.

138. New York Daily News Building, New York, 1930. Hood and Howells; Raymond Hood, designer. Eight years after the Chicago Tribune tower, Hood designed another newspaper skyscraper, with very different results.

139. Drexel Bank, Philadelphia, 1927. Charles Z. Klauder. Fifteenth-century Florence, home of the Medicis, supplied the inspiration for this bank building—which also owes something, most likely, to McKim's University Club in New York.

140. Interborough Rapid Transit Company powerhouses, New York, 1902. Stanford White, designer of exterior. White donated his design services for the "facework" that screens vast arrays of boilers, bunkers, compound engines, and dynamos.

141. New York Telephone (Barclay-Vesey) Building, New York, finished 1926. Voorhees, Gmelin and Walker; Ralph Walker, designer. An early Art Deco skyscraper, with delicate ground-floor detailing in marked contrast to its heaven-storming masses, that was much admired in the late twenties.

142. Study for a concrete skyscraper, ca. 1929. Hugh Ferriss, designer and renderer. Ferriss was much in demand as a renderer in the twenties; a visionary, he foresaw an Americanized *ville radieuse* in *The Metropolis of Tomorrow* (1929).

143. "Spadina House," Beverly Hills, Cal., 1925. Henry Oliver. Some of the poetic wretchedness of this extraordinary house was designed into it, but it is hard to believe that it always looked as decayed as in this recent photograph.

144. Nationality Room in the Cathedral of Learning, Pittsburgh, 1930s. This Gothic skyscraper contains seventeen classrooms in different national styles, plus an eighteenth-century library from Damascus and a Greek Revival ballroom from a Pittsburgh mansion. This is the Swedish Classroom.

145. Grauman's Metropolitan Theatre, Los Angeles, 1923: promenade under balcony. William Lee Woollett. In the decade that saw the spread of the monster movie house, Grauman's Metropolitan won special attention, partly for the use of exposed concrete under the grand stair.

146.   Illustration by Robert Osborn for Elizabeth B. Mock, *If You Want to Build a House*. "Encouraging" the Eclectic's clientele to go modern.

147.   Federal Reserve Bank, Philadelphia, 1932–34. Paul Crét. Such compromise classicism often appeared in official and institutional architecture from the late twenties on.

"Architecture, literature and sentimentality becomes hopelessly confused."

148.   House in Needham, Mass., ca. 1940. Royal Barry Wills. Wills was a popular Eclectic of the 1930s and '40s, specializing in houses, who retained a mastery of proportion and detail; among other styles in his repertoire was a mild form of the International Style.

149.   The Capitol, Williamsburg, reconstructed ca. 1932. The American taste for replicas and reconstructed historical sites, in the absence of authentic remains, reveals a fondness for make-believe that is one of the components of Electicism.

WILLIAMSBURG® Shell Pattern . . . the new Stieff sterling silver reproduction is based on an assembled set of English Georgian flatware in the Williamsburg Collection. Under strict supervision of Colonial Williamsburg, and adhering to rigid standards of quality, Stieff craftsmen spent five years creating this new sterling silver pattern. It combines the graceful shell motif— one of man's oldest decorative symbols —with the Williamsburg Hallmark.

The original flatware dates from 1760 when four-tined forks were coming into fashion, and bold pistol-handle knives reflected the flourish with which Colonial Americans lived. The authenticity of this beautiful reproduction is flawless. And, its timeliness is enhanced by the approach of our nation's two-hundredth birthday. See this exciting new Stieff sterling silver pattern at fine jewelry and department stores. Or, write for literature.

Stieff Co.

800 Wyman Park Drive
Baltimore, Maryland 21211

Introducing...
WILLIAMSBURG®
Shell Pattern...
a new sterling silver
reproduction by Stieff

®Identifies Trademarks owned by The Colonial Williamsburg Foundation, Reg. U.S. Pat. Off.

150. Advertisement for Colonial Williamsburg reproductions. 1973. High-quality reproductions of Colonial furnishings and decorative materials are still in demand.

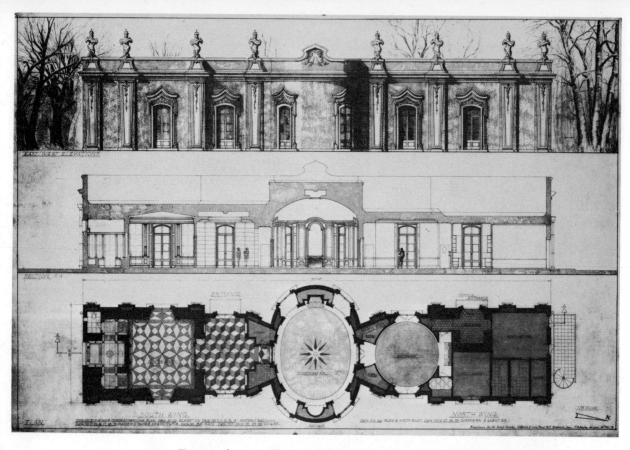

151. Design for a villa in Greenwich, Conn., 1958. John Barrington Bayley. Modern Eclecticism: a pavilion-like house in the Barocchetto ("little Baroque") of early eighteenth-century Italy, finished in stucco painted oyster-white against ultramarine.

152. Trompe-l'oeil interior in New York, ca. 1970. Hight Moore, decorator. Interior decoration, rather than architecture, carries on the spirit of Eclecticism today.

Notes

What Was Eclecticism?

1. John Maass offers a selection of latter-day Independence Halls in "Architecture and Americanism, or Pastiches of Independence Hall," *Charette*, September/October 1969.

2. One reason why the Stockholm City Hall was not imitated over here was probably its specifically Nordic quality, but another must have been the formidable cost of the materials and workmanship Östberg put into the building.

3. Two good surveys published during the 1920s offer many illustrations of Eclectic buildings and give a good intelligently worded expression of Eclectic attitudes. These are Talbot F. Hamlin, *The American Spirit in Architecture* (Yale University, 1926), a general picture history of American architecture, but with some 440 of his illustrations devoted to Eclectic architecture, and G. H. Edgell, *The American Architecture of To-day* (Scribner's, 1928).

Thomas A. Tallmadge, in *The Story of Architecture in America* (Norton, 1927), presents Eclectic attitudes once again, which are all the more interesting because he was once a Prairie School architect; indeed, one chapter, "Louis Sullivan and the Lost Cause," has gained a certain notoriety.

C. Matlack Price, *The Practical Book of Architecture* (Lippincott, 1916) explains architecture to those about to build, revealing attitudes common at the time.

Werner Hegemann and Albert Peets, *The American Vitruvius: An Architect's Handbook of Civic Art* (Architectural Book Publishing Co., 1922) is very good on city planning and large-scale projects.

W. A. Starrett, *Skyscrapers and the Men Who Build Them* (Scribner's, 1928) is excellent on the state of the building art.

More recent surveys are sometimes openly hostile to Eclecticism, sometimes quietly disapproving. Henry-Russell Hitchcock, *Architecture: Nineteenth and Twentieth Centuries* (Penguin, 1958) gives limited space to the Eclectics but is probably the most objective. You may wish also to consult John Burchard and Albert Bush-Brown, *The Architecture of America: A Social and Cultural History* (abridged edition, Little, Brown, 1966) and William H. Jordy, *Progressive and Academic Ideals at the Turn of the Twentieth Century* (Doubleday, 1972). Marcus Whiffen, *American Architecture Since 1780: A Guide to the Styles* (M.I.T., 1969) attempts to classify the various forms of Eclecticism. See also Walter C. Kidney, "Another Look at Eclecticism," *Progressive Architecture*, September 1967.

Two anthologies of writings from the Eclectic period should also be mentioned: Montgomery Schuyler, *American Architecture and Other Writings,* ed. William H. Jordy (Belknap Press, 1961) and Henry Van Brunt, *Architecture and Society: Selected Essays of Henry van Brunt,* ed. William A. Coles (Harvard, 1969).

There are numerous architectural guides and histories for specific cities and regions that supplement this general background reading. Particularly interesting are Bainbridge Bunting, *Houses of Boston's Back Bay: An Architectural History 1840–1917* (Belknap Press, 1967); Scully's section of Antoinette F. Downing and Vincent Scully, *The Architectural Heritage of Newport, R. I.* (second edition, revised, Potter, 1967; henceforth Scully, *Newport*); W. Hawkins Ferry, *The Buildings of Detroit: A History* (Wayne State, 1968); Roger Olmsted and T. H. Watkins, *Here Today: San Francisco's Architectural Heritage* (Chronicle Books [San Francisco], 1968); and three architectural guides, Norval White and Elliot Wilensky, *AIA Guide to New York City* (Macmillan, 1968); Richard Longstreth and Edward Teitelman, *The Architecture of Philadelphia* (M.I.T., 1974); and James Van Trump and Arthur Ziegler, *Landmark Architecture of Allegheny County Pennsylvania* (Pittsburgh History and Landmarks Foundation, 1967).

The Nightmare of the Eclectics

4. Edgell, Hamlin, Tallmadge, and many others go on at length about the vicious state of American architecture in the mid-Victorian period; in the mythos of the 1920s, Richardson and Hunt were no less than messengers of light. Until quite recently, of course, modernists had no higher opinion of Victorian architecture, seeing it, when they saw it at all, as a fungoid growth on Victorian construction.

5. Bunting, *Houses of Boston's Back Bay*, is very interesting on design and construction practices, and the profession generally, in the mid-Victorian period.

6. This, of course, is mid-Victorian architecture and design as seen by the Eclectics. Consider, on the other hand, John Maass, *The Gingerbread Age* (Rinehart, 1957) and *The Victorian Home in America* (Hawthorn, 1972), which give a sympathetic view. For the mid-Victorian interior, see Harold L. Peterson, *Americans at Home: From the Colonists to the Late Victorians* (Scribner's, 1971), which interprets it on the evidence of photographs and other contemporary pictures, and the illustrated catalogue by Berry B. Tracy *et al.*, *Nineteenth-Century America: Furniture and Other Decorative Arts* (Metropolitan Museum [New York], 1970).

The mid-Victorian architects published many books of designs for builders and their clients, with copious texts; see for example the books of Samuel Sloan, Calvert Vaux, John Riddell, Marcus Cummings and Charles Miller, George Woodward, and Frederick Withers.

And the Awakening: the Aesthetic Period

7. *Hints* was reprinted recently (Dover, 1969).

8. See Bruce J. Talbert, *Gothic Forms* (American edition, James R. Osgood and Co., 1873) and *Examples of Ancient and Modern Furniture* (American edition, James R. Osgood and Co., 1877).

9. For the Aesthetic period in England, see Elizabeth Aslin, *The Aesthetic Movement: Prelude to Art Nouveau* (Praeger, 1969).

10. For Japanese influence, see Aslin, *op. cit.*, and Clay Lancaster, *The Japanese Influence in America* (Walton H. Rawls, n.d.).

11. "Shavian Manorial" is Henry-Russell Hitchcock's label. Not everyone accepts it, but it does seem useful to distinguish between the half-timbered Tudoresque Queen Anne and the quasi-Carolean brick Queen Anne.

12. Colonial Revival does not have its monograph yet, though it surely will soon. But Scully touches on it both in *Shingle Style*, cited below, and *Newport;* John Calvin Stevens and Albert Winslow Cobb, in *Examples*, cited below, show their early work in the style; and Walter Knight Sturges, in "Arthur Little and the Colonial Revival," JSAH XXXII, 2 (May 1973) discusses the work of an important Colonial Revival architect.

13. Other interesting books from the Aesthetic period include Henry Hudson Holly, *Modern Dwellings in Town and Country* (Harper's, 1878), Harriett Prescott Spofford, *Art Decoration Applied to Furniture* (Harper's, 1878), and Clarence Cook, *The House Beautiful* (Scribner's, 1881). The whole of JSAH XXXII, 2 (May 1973) is devoted to late Victorian architecture in the important Boston area and should be examined.

14. On the Shingle Style, see Vincent J. Scully, Jr., *The Stick Style and the Shingle Style* (Yale, 1971; henceforth, *Shingle Style*); John Calvin Stevens and Albert Winslow Cobb, *Examples of American Domestic Architecture* (William T. Comstock, 1889); and Cynthia Zaitevsky, *The Architecture of William Ralph Emerson, 1833–1917* (Fogg Art Museum, 1969).

15. See James D. Kornwolf, *M. H. Baillie Scott and the Arts and Crafts Movement* (Johns Hopkins, 1972) for Shingle Style influence in England. See Arnold Lewis, "Hinckeldyn, Vogel, and American Architecture," JSAH XXXI, 4 (December 1972) for Shingle Style influence in Germany. Swedish biographies of Ragnar Östberg and Carl Westman, both of whom spent time in the United States, show houses of theirs influenced by the Shingle Style.

Ideas and Education

16. Techniques for graphic reproduction of architecture have been influenced by and influential on the aesthetic values of different periods. The Greek Revival, a neatly edged style with no interest in textures, was represented in the builder's guides of Lafever and Benjamin in copper plate, but the Romantic architects from about 1845 through the early 1860s favored chromolithography when they could afford it. Downing's books, no doubt because they were intended to be cheap, used wood engravings, as did other octavos of the 1850s for the mass market. By 1870, when architecture was temporarily dry and linear, engraving and lithographs in outline, without shading, were again favored. Around this same time photo reproduction of line drawings began to offer an alternative to hand engraving; the latter had become extremely competent, but the former allowed the artist's touch to be reproduced exactly, and came to be preferred for architectural publications. With the growing interest in textures and curved surfaces the line technique became freer, to suggest shingles, fieldstone, and highlights on modeled forms.

One of the things that had contributed to the "Victorian" look of mid-Victorian architecture was its lack of faithful reproductions of Euorpean architecture; measured drawings reproduced in engravings, engraved or lithographed perspectives were all that books of that time had to offer, and these either suppressed or distorted important aspects of their subjects. Early methods for reproducing photographs, sharp but expensive, had to be used sparingly. When the modern halftone process came into general use in the eighties it gained a fair amount of acceptance, despite its initial crudities; it coexisted with line cuts until the early nineties, when it became cheap and reliable enough to replace them entirely.

See Scully, *Shingle Style*, note 35, p. 10; Eileen Michels, "Late Nineteenth-Century Published American Perspective Drawing," JSAH XXXI, 4 (December 1972), with drawings by Harvey Ellis and Henry P. Kirby, mentioned below.

17. William Rotch Ware, the first editor of *American Architect*, was regarded by the Eclectics as one of the most important and benign influences on American architecture. The magazine included photographs from the start— good but expensive collotype prints for the first ten years, halftones after the mid-eighties.

18. The first head of the M.I.T. school was William Robert Ware, who had studied with Richard Morris Hunt at the Tenth Street Studio (see text, below) and who was a relative of William Rotch Ware.

19. See, for example, *Palliser's Model Homes: Showing a Variety of Designs for Model Dwellings* (1878; reprint Glenwood Publishers [Felton, Cal.], 1972), especially interesting for its descriptions of color schemes.

20. For Aesthetic interiors around 1880, see Anon., *Artistic Houses* (Appleton, ca. 1883–85; reprinted Benjamin Blom, 1971). See also Robert Koch, *Louis C. Tiffany: Rebel in Glass* (Crown, 1966).

Richardson

21. Thus far, there are only two books on Richardson: Marianna Griswold van Rensselaer, *Henry Hobson Richardson and His Works* (1888; reprinted Prairie School Press [Palos Park, Ill.], 1967, and Dover, 1969) and Henry-Russell Hitchcock, *The Architecture of H. H. Richardson and His Times* (revised edition Archon Books [Hamden, Conn.], 1961). Both should be read. The Van Rensselaer must be the first of the great folio monographs on American architects.

22. On the Watts Sherman house, see Scully, *Shingle Style*.

23. See Harold Kirker and David van Zanten, "Jean Lemoulnier in Boston," JSAH XXXI, 3 (October 1972).

24. See George L. Wrenn, "'A Return to Solid and Classical Principles': Arthur D. Gilman, 1859," JSAH XX, 4 (December 1961).

25. Mid-Victorian architecture can show many buildings, churches, schools, and rural houses especially, of roughly dressed stone or rubble, but one feels that the textured surfaces resulting were a concession to economy rather than a matter of preference. The edges are kept hard, and the patterns created by porches, cornices, window frames, etc., keep the rough wall material firmly in its place.

26. For LaFarge, see Royal Cortissoz, *John LaFarge: A Memoir and a Study* (Houghton Mifflin, 1913; reprinted Da Capo, 1971). For LaFarge at Trinity, see Van Brunt, *Architecture and Society* (Harvard, 1969).

27. See Theodore E. Stebbins, Jr., "Richardson and Trinity Church: The Evolution of a Building," JSAH XXVII, 4 (December 1968).

28. Lewis Mumford celebrates this Richardson in *Sticks and Stones* (Boni and Liveright, 1924) and *The Brown Decades* (Harcourt Brace and Co., 1931).

29. Hitchcock, interested in Richardson the modernist, almost always deplores his ornament.

30. For Richardson the correspondent see Marc Friedlaender, "Henry Hobson Richardson, Henry Adams, and John Hay," JSAH XXIX, 3 (October 1970).

31. An unbiased look at the commercial architecture of the mid-eighties, including that by Sullivan and Root, suggests that the great façades, which could be acres in area, presented an embarrassment rather than an opportunity. Eclectics spoke of the "treatment" of a large façade, as if it constituted some sort of medical emergency.

32. Richardson had some influence in northern Europe too. See Leonard Eaton, *American Architecture Comes of Age* (M.I.T., 1972).

33. For Harvey Ellis, see the *Prairie School Review* V, 1–2 (a Harvey Ellis double edition; first-second quarter, 1968).

Hunt

34. There is no book on Hunt, strangely enough, but Schuyler, *American Architecture* and Van Brunt, *Architecture and Society,* include essays on him. See also Alan Burnham, "The New York Architecture of Richard Morris Hunt," JSAH XI, 2 (May 1952) and Scully, *Newport.*

35. A few wealthy families had houses faced in marble before this time, but the center of the American city was predominantly red and brown.

Post; Price

36. These two architects also have had surprisingly skimpy coverage, at least in recent times. Winston Weisman, "The Commercial Architecture of George B. Post," JSAH XXXI, 3 (October 1972) is perhaps the only good source on Post, and Price—as a Shingle Style architect—is discussed in Scully, *Shingle Style.*

McKim, Mead and White

37. The firm is rather well documented. For its work, see the four-volume *Monograph of the Work of McKim, Mead and White 1879–1915* (Architectural Book Publishing Co., 1915), or the much more modest survey of Charles H. Reilly, *McKim, Mead and White* (Ernest Benn [London], 1924; reprinted Benjamin Blom, 1972). For McKim see especially Charles H. Moore, *The Life and Times of Charles Follen McKim* (Houghton Mifflin, 1929); or, as an alternative, Alfred Hoyt Granger, *Charles Follen McKim: A Study of His Life and Work* (Houghton Mifflin, 1913; reprinted Benjamin Blom, 1972). White is warmly portrayed in Charles C. Baldwin, *Stanford White* (Dodd, Mead, 1931) with its loquacious index.

38. 1872 is Scully's date; Sturges, *op. cit.*, our note 12, gives 1875.

39. White had been dissuaded from a career as a painter by John LaFarge.

40. For illustrations of the Newport Casino and the "Kingscote" dining room see Scully, *Shingle Style* or *Newport*.

41. Wells is the subject of an appendix in Baldwin, *Stanford White*.

42. The eighteen-foot-high *Diana* Saint-Gaudens created to adorn the tower of Madison Square Garden was found to be overscaled, so at their own expense White and Saint-Gaudens had her replaced with a version thirteen feet high. The first *Diana* thereupon went to Chicago, first to McKim, Mead and White's Agricultural Building at the World's Columbian Exposition as a finial for the dome, then to the Montgomery Ward Building as a weathervane; the second *Diana* is now in the stair hall of the Philadelphia Museum of Art.

Expensive architectural revisions of this sort happened now and then, and form part of the folklore of Eclecticism. Richardson would tear down walls he found dull. When the terra cotta work for the Madison Square Presbyterian Church was first set up, White found it too regular and had it reset with artful carelessness. McKim paid for the replacement of a column in which he had detected an almost imperceptible flaw. Addison Mizner moved walls or had them breached with windows to improve the composition. Thomas Hastings, dissatisfied with the entrance block of the New York Public Library, is said to have bequeathed money to have the corners altered—though this was never done.

The Grand Scale

43. The World's Columbian Exposition was well illustrated at the time; with the development of the halftone process, picture books had begun to emerge in large numbers, and the fair was an obvious subject. J. W. Buel, *The Magic City* (Historical Publishing Co. [St. Louis and Philadelphia], 1894) is perhaps the best.

44. Figure 40 shows the following: in the foreground, Daniel Chester French's statue of the Republic. From the left, around the Basin: Agriculture Building (McKim, Mead and White, New York); Mechanical Arts Building (Peabody and Stearns, Boston); Administration Building (Richard Morris Hunt, New York); Electricity Building (Van Brunt and Howe, Kansas City, but originally Boston); Manufactures Building (George B. Post, New York). The view is taken from the Peristyle and Triumphal Arch (Charles B. Atwood, Chicago but until very recently New York). Ergo, all the above architects were Easterners.

45. On Burnham, see Charles H. Moore, *Daniel H. Burnham: Architect, Planner of Cities* (Houghton Mifflin, 1921). On the very sore point of the fair as a defeat for progressive American architecture and Burnham's role in that defeat, see first Sullivan's wrathful comments in *The Autobiography of an Idea* (Press of the American Institute of Architects, 1922), then two essays from JSAH XXVI, 4 (December 1967): David H. Crook, "Louis Sullivan and the Golden Doorway" and Dmitri Tselos, "The Chicago Fair and the Myth of the 'Lost Cause'"; and, from JSAH XXIX, 3 (October 1970), Titus M. Karlowicz, "D. H. Burnham's Role in the Selection of Architects for the World's Columbian Exposition."

The Beaux-Arts Style

46. For the St. Louis Exposition see a picture book by Walter B. Stevens, *The Forest City* (N. D. Thompson Publishing Co. [St. Louis], 1904). The Beaux-Arts style has not yet had the study it deserves.

47. The Philadelphia City Hall took so long to build (1874–94) that its Second Empire style went out of, then somewhat back into, fashion during its construction.

48. See his Scribner Building, Figure 74.

"The Scale is Roman, and It Will Have to Be Sustained" (McKim)

49. Henry Hope Reed, Jr. praises the City Beautiful and its architecture in *The Golden City* (Doubleday, 1959) and in "The Vision Spurned: Classical New York," *Classical America*, I, 1 and 2.

50. For Washington, see John W. Reps, *Monumental Washington* (Princeton, 1967) and Moore's biographies of Burnham and McKim, *op. cit.*

51. For Chicago, see Daniel H. Burnham and Edward H. Bennett, *Plan of Chicago* (The Commercial Club [Chicago], 1909; reprinted Da Capo, 1970), as well as Moore's biography of Burnham.

52. For the Parkway, see George B. Tatum, *Penn's Great Town* (U. of Pennsylvania, 1961) and George and Mary Roberts, *Triumph on Fairmount: Fiske Kimball and the Philadelphia Museum of Art* (Lippincott, 1959).

53. For Guastavino's contribution to Eclectic architecture see George R. Collins, "The Transfer of Thin Masonry Vaulting from Spain to America," JSAH XXVII, 3 (October 1968).

54. Or, alternatively, as a classical composition with a beginning, a middle, and an end.

The Eclectic and the Engineer

55. On ship interiors, see Douglas Phillips-Birt, *When Luxury Went to Sea* (St. Martin's, 1971); John Malcolm Brinnin, *The Sway of the Grand Saloon* (Delacorte, 1971); or John Maxtone-Graham, *The Only Way to Cross* (Macmillan, 1972).

56. For the Eclectic-engineer situation see Wilbur J. Watson, *Bridge Architecture* (William Helburn, 1927), Charles Evan Fowler, *The Ideals of Engineering Architecture* (Gilette Publishing Co., 1929), or Francis S. Onderdonk, *The Ferro-Concrete Style* (Architectural Book Publishing Co., 1928).

57. Cass Gilbert had designed a simple casing of ashlar for the towers of the George Washington Bridge in New York. When this was left off, functionalists rejoiced, although it appears that, from a strictly utilitarian, as opposed to a functionalist, viewpoint the matter was indifferent: the money saved has been spent on keeping the exposed steelwork painted.

Collaborators (1)

58. The Hunt debacle is related, among other places, in Pierce Rice, "The Missing Ingredient," *Classical America*, I, 2. For the muralists, see Edwin Howland Blashfield, *Mural Painting in America* (Scribner's, 1914). Interesting, too, are the Rice articles cited above; Royal Cortissoz, *American Artists* (Scribner's 1923), Homer Saint-Gaudens, *The American Artist and His Times* (Dodd, Mead, 1940); and Henry C. Pitz, *The Brandywine Tradition* (Houghton Mifflin, 1968).

59. An excellent general history is Wayne Craven's *Sculpture in America* (Crowell, 1968). See also the Cortissoz and Homer Saint-Gaudens works cited above.

60. See James M. Dennis, *Karl Bitter: Architectural Sculptor, 1867–1915* (Wisconsin, 1967).

61. See Louise Hall Tharp, *Saint-Gaudens and the Gilded Era* (Little Brown, 1970).

62. See Adeline Adams, *Daniel Chester French: Sculptor* (Houghton Mifflin, 1932).

63. See Edwin Murtha, *Paul Manship* (Macmillan, 1957).

64. Jordy, in *Progressive and Academic Ideals*, discusses Burnham and his office system; so does Moore, in his biography. Moore also discusses Atwood.

65. For tramp draftsmen, see William Gray Purcell, "This, Too, Might Be History," JSAH III, 4 (October 1943).

The Second Generation

66. For Gilbert, see his *Cass Gilbert: Reminiscences and Addresses* (Private printing, Scribner's Press, 1935).

67. For Hastings, see David Gray, *Thomas Hastings, Architect* (Houghton Mifflin, 1935).

68. Brown is discussed, with warm approval, in Reed, *The Golden City*.

69. A chapter is devoted to Maybeck in Esther McCoy, *Five California Architects* (Praeger, 1960).

70. For Hornbostel, see Van Trump and Ziegler, *Landmark Architecture of Allegheny County Pennsylvania*, and James Van Trump and Barry Hannegan, "The Stones of Carnegie Tech," *Charette*, September 1958.

71. Outside the College of Fine Arts a blind wall screens an art gallery and a small Louis XVI theater ("Ici l'inspiration deploye ses ailes"); in this wall are five deep niches, which were to be carved with ornament in the Gothic, Greek, Roman, Renaissance, and Persian manners. The Italian stonecutter, having made a start on the Roman and Renaissance niches, returned home to join the colors when war broke out and never returned. Inside, the main corridor floor, of white marble, is inlaid in verde antique with the plans of Michelangelo's design for St. Peter's, the Parthenon, the cathedral of Chartres, and an Egyptian temple. The vaults are painted with pastel views of famous buildings, cameo-like paintings of famous sculptures, portrait medallions of great artists, and the tunes of famous musical compositions. An office on the main axis is framed in a cast from Puget's entrance to the Hôtel de Ville at Toulon.

72. Pope's work is shown in Royal Cortissoz, *The Architecture of John Russell Pope* (W. Helburn, Inc., 1924–1928).

73. Magazines of the period include *American Architect and Building News* (1876–1938); *Architectural Forum* (1917–present, with interruptions); *Architectural Record* (1891–present); *Architectural Review* (Boston; 1891–1921); *Brickbuilder* (1892–1916; became *Architectural Forum*); *Pencil Points* (1920–1945; became *Progressive Architecture*). These are national magazines. There are more local magazines, such as *Inland Architect, Western Architect,* and *Charette* (Pittsburgh).

The Panama-Pacific Exposition, 1915

74. For the Panama-Pacific, see Louis Christian Mullgardt *et al.*, *The Architecture and Landscape Gardening of the Exposition* (Paul Elder and Co. [San Francisco], 1915); Eugen Neuhaus, *The Art of the Exposition* (Paul Elder and Co., 1915); John D. Barry, *The City of Domes* (John J. Newbegin [San Francisco], 1915); and Bernard R. Maybeck, *Palace of Fine Arts and Lagoon* (Paul Elder and Co., 1915).

The Home

75. The evolving Neo-Georgian acquired a kind of ideology from Joy Wheeler Dow in *American Renaissance* (William T. Comstock [New York], 1904); brisk, dogmatic, not unlikable, Dow stressed the "Anglo-Saxon home atmosphere" found in Colonial and Early Federal work. Like classicists of all times—Berenson in our time, for instance—he held originality in little esteem, regarding it as permissible once the eternal values were understood rather than as a *sine qua non* of art.

76. In her novels, Edith Wharton showed a feeling for architecture. The protagonist of *The Age of Innocence*, a rich and semi-intellectual New Yorker of the mid-1870s, allows his young bride to furnish their house in the conventional mid-Victorian way as long as he can have an Eastlake library with "sincere" furniture and sliding curtains. In *Hudson River Bracketed* (1929) her young Midwestern writer's happiness at discovering the cultural past is symbolized by hours in a villa of the 1840s (whose ornamentation, as the 1920s would wish, is mercifully obscured by foliage).

77. For Platt, see Royal Cortissoz, *Monograph of the Work of Charles A. Platt* (Architectural Book Publishing Co., 1913).

78. *American Country Houses of To-day* (Architectural Book Publishing Co.) was the annual. Other books of interest include Charles Edwin Hooper, *The Country House* (Doubleday Page and Co., 1906); Barr Ferree, *American Estates and Gardens* (Munn and Co., 1906).

79. Henry M. Saylor, *Bungalows* (John C. Winston Co. [Philadelphia], 1911); Albert Bradlee Hunt, ed., *Houseboats and Houseboating* (Forest and Stream Publishing Co., 1905).

80. Aladdin Homes and similar prefabricated houses of the 1915 period were essentially kits for local carpenters; they included all lumber, cut to size; hardware; fastenings; building paper; shingles or composition roofing; glass;

wood finishes; putty; lath and plaster or plasterboard. Furnaces, plumbing, and electrical fixtures were sold as extras. Masonry and wiring had to be arranged separately.

The Mild Innovators

81. For Scheibler, see Van Trump and Ziegler, *Landmark Architecture of Allegheny County Pennsylvania*; John Knox Shear and Robert W. Schmertz, "A Pittsburgh Original," *Charette*, September 1948; and James Van Trump, "A Prophet of Modern Architecture in Pittsburgh: Frederick G. Scheibler, Jr.," *Charette*, October 1962.

82. For Mullgardt's houses, see Anonymous, "An Architectural Innovator," *Architectural Record*, XXX, 2 (August 1911). For the Court of Ages, see Robert J. Clark, "Louis Christian Mullgardt and the Court of the Ages," JSAH XXI, 4 (December 1962).

83. Bragdon's only executed design of any fame was the New York Central station at Rochester, now demolished; opened in 1910, it used a simple geometrical system of proportion, but its quasi-classical ornament was not derived from mathematical formulas. Bragdon's most important architectural works are *The Beautiful Necessity* (Knopf, 1922); *Projective Ornament* (Manas Press [Rochester N.Y.] 1915); *Architecture and Democracy* (Knopf, 1918); and *The Frozen Fountain* (Knopf, 1932). See also his autobiography, *More Lives Than One* (Knopf, 1938). There are also mystical books and a book of theatrical memoirs.

The Gothic

84. Architects in Charleston appear to have used decorative terra-cotta in thé 1850s for window caps and similar details; frost would not have been a severe problem. On the introduction of terra-cotta to the United States generally, see Margaret Henderson Floyd, "A Terra-Cotta Cornerstone for Copley Square: Museum of Fine Arts, Boston, 1870–1876, by Sturgis and Brigham," JSAH XXXII, 2 (May 1973). See also, Harley J. McKee, *Introduction to Early American Masonry* (National Trust and Columbia University, 1973).

85. On Richardson's cathedral, see Montgomery Schuyler, "An American Cathedral," in *American Architecture*, cited above.

86. On St. John the Divine, see Edward Hagaman Hall, *et al.*, *A Guide to the Cathedral Church of St. John the Divine* (Pub. by the dean and chapter, 1965); James Marston Fitch, "At Peace with the Past: The Unfinished Church," in *Architecture and the Esthetics of Plenty* (Columbia, 1961); and Cram, *My Life in Architecture* (Little, Brown 1936).

87. Wood (1855–97) is best known for his Peddie Memorial Baptist Church in Newark, Romanesque like much of his work, and for the fantastic "Jerusalem the Golden" design for St. John the Divine. Information on him is not very accessible: Florence Wood, *Memories of William Halsey Wood, Written by His Wife* (Mrs. William Halsey Wood [Philadelphia] 1938) or James Van Trump, "Pittsburgh's Church of the Ascension," *Charette*, June 1956.

Cram

88. For Cram, see his own works, particularly *Church Building* (Marshall, Jones and Co., [Boston], 1899; 1914; 1924); *The Gothic Quest* (Baker and Taylor [New York], 1907); and *My Life in Architecture*. See also the folio *The Work of Cram and Ferguson, Architects* (Pencil Points Press, 1929) or the small monograph *Ralph Adams Cram* (Whittlesey House [McGraw-Hill], 1931) in the Whittlesey House Contemporary American Architects series.

89. *My Life in Architecture* dwells on these matters. It is interesting to see Cram favoring Mussolini, presumably because Mussolini was said to be reviving the guild system.

90. Cram, *My Life in Architecture*.

Goodhue

91. See Charles Whitaker, *et al.*, *Bertram Grosvenor Goodhue: Architect and Master of Many Arts* (Press of the American Institute of Architects, 1925). Cram discusses Goodhue and their partnership in *My Life in Architecture*.

92. For the Panama-California Exposition, see Bertram Grosvenor Goodhue, *et al.*, *The Architecture and Gardens of the San Diego Exposition* (Paul Elder and Co., 1916) or Eugen Neuhaus, *The San Diego Garden Fair* (Paul Elder and Co., 1916).

. . . and Others

93. For the Eclectic church and synagogue, see Ralph Adams Cram, ed., *American Church Building of To-day* (Architectural Book Publishing Co., 1929). For the general work of the architects mentioned here, see Edgell and Hamlin, and the yearbooks of the Architectural League of New York, the Boston Architectural Club, and the T-Square Club (Philadelphia).

94. There had been plenty of mid-Victorian academic Gothic, of course. Eclectic academic Gothic can perhaps be dated from Cope and Stewardson's Tudor work at Bryn Mawr, starting with Denbigh Hall in 1891.

For academic Eclecticism, see Charles Z. Klauder and Herbert C. Wise, *College Architecture in America* (Scribner's, 1929).

Commercial Gothic

95. The Tribune competition is recorded, with many pictures, in *Chicago Tribune, The International Competition for a New Administration Building for the Chicago Tribune*, MCMXXII (1922)—a curious assortment of designs.

The Romantic Suburb

96. For Furness, see James F. O'Gorman, *The Architecture of Frank Furness* (Philadelphia Museum of Art, 1973).

97. Eyre is another neglected figure, although Louis Kornwolf mentions him in *M. H. Baillie Scott and the Arts and Crafts Movement*, as does Scully in *Shingle Style*. The best study is an early one, Alfred Morton Githens, "Wilson Eyre Jr.: His Work," *Architectural Annual* for 1900. A look at Howard Pyle's versions of Robin Hood or the King Arthur stories, or at any Maxfield Parrish work where an architectural setting appears, will confirm the parallel made here even though Eyre designed houses rather than castles.

98. There are two folio monographs on these architects: Owen Wister *et al.*, *A Monograph of the Work of Mellor Meigs and Howe* (Architectural Book Publishing Co., 1923) and *Monograph of the Work of Robert R. McGoodwin* (William F. Fell, Co., Printers [Philadelphia], 1942). See also Willard S. Detweiler, Jr., Inc., *Chestnut Hill: An Architectural History* (Philadelphia: Chestnut Hill Historical Society, 1969), and Edward Teitelman and Richard W. Longstreth, *Architecture in Philadelphia*.

The Latin Styles

99. For the Latin styles generally, see two books by Rexford Newcomb, *The Spanish House for America* (Lippincott, 1927) and *Mediterranean Domestic Architecture of the United States* (Janson [Cleveland], 1928).

100. For Mizner, see Ida M. Tarbell, *The Florida Architecture of Addison Mizner* (William Helburn, 1928); Alva M. Johnston, *The Legendary Mizners* (Farrar, Straus and Young, 1953); and Addison Mizner, *The Many Mizners* (Sears Publishing Co., 1932). A book by the present author is in preparation.

101. The Pueblo Style is illustrated in Marcus Whiffen, *American Architecture Since 1780*.

Collaborators (II)

102. Cram, *My Life in Architecture*, discusses the craftsmen and artists he worked with; Whitaker, *Bertram Grosvenor Goodhue*, includes a memoir by Lee Lawrie on his collaborations with Goodhue.

103. See Koch, *Louis Comfort Tiffany*, for the controversy over the principles of stained-glass design. For Yellin, see Myra Tolmach Davis, "Samuel Yellin's Sketches in Iron," *Historic Preservation*, October, 1971.

104. A brief history of the White Pine Series is given in Charles Magruder, "The White Pine Monograph Series," JSAH XXII, 1 (March 1963); see also John F. Harbeson, "Stotham, The Massachusetts Hoax, 1920," JSAH XXIII, 2 (May 1964).

Draftsmen's guides, catalogues, periodicals distributed by materials suppliers, and books published by trade organizations are numerous. To name but a few: a guide, *Architectural Terra Cotta: Standard Construction* (The National Terra Cotta Society, U.S.A., 1914); an *Illustrated Catalogue of Plastic Ornaments* (The Decorators Supply Company, Chicago, ca. 1903; including "Sullivanesque" ornament); a catalogue of *Interior and Exterior Decorative Ornament* (The Fischer and Jirouch Company, Cleveland, 1931); every other month, the *White Pine Series of Architectural Monographs* (the White Pine Bureau, 1915–40); the *Tuileries Brochures* (Ludowici-Celadon Company, tile manufacturers in Chicago, 1929–32); *Atlantic Terra Cotta* (the

Atlantic Terra Cotta Company, New York, 1913–18, 1921–32); and an annual, *New York Plaisance* (Henry Erkins Studios, decorators and decorative supply manufacturers of New York, 1908). Among the books are two published by the American Face Brick Association, *English Precedent for Modern Brickwork* (1924) and *Brickwork in Italy* (1925).

The Grandeur of the State

105. For government architecture at the county and municipal levels, see R. W. Sexton, ed., *American Public Buildings of To-day* (Architectural Book Publishing Co., 1931). An architectural and historical survey of the state capitols is under preparation by Henry-Russell Hitchcock and William Seale.

106. An interesting aspect of the Cleveland Federal Building was Arnold Brunner's erection on the site of a full-scale mockup of a bay, in staff, to determine the effect; it is reproduced in *Architectural Record*, XXIX, 3 (March 1911).

107. Trumbauer's Free Library building in Philadelphia (Fig. 76) is an example.

108. The state-capitol dome goes back at least as far as the capitol building at Annapolis, built in the 1770s.

Apogee

109. For Albert Kahn, see W. Hawkins Ferry, *et al.*, *The Legacy of Albert Kahn* (Detroit Institute of Arts, 1970) and Ferry, *The Buildings of Detroit.*

110. As Hitchcock noted in *Modern Architecture: Romanticism and Reintegration* (1929; reprinted Hacker, 1970).

The Post–1916 Skyscraper

111. For the business building of the 1920s, see R. W. Sexton, *American Commercial Buildings of To-day* (Architectural Book Publishing Co., 1928).

112. These extravagances did occur, however. The Chicago Tribune has a crown of buttresses, and the Cathedral of Learning in Pittsburgh has pointed windows with tracery several stories high. The blind, encrusted tops and occasional steep roofs of many skyscrapers were more rational, since they concealed machinery and water tanks.

113. Even modernists liked the Shelton; Mumford, Sheldon Cheney, and Hugh Ferriss had good words for it despite its traditional ornament.

114. See Ferry, *The Buildings of Detroit.*

115. For Howells, see Anonymous, *John Mead Howells* (Architectural Catalog Co., Printer, n.d.).

Industry and New Materials

116. Albert Kahn produced some of the most successfully ornamented industrial buildings, but they still have a contrived look.

117. The functionalism of railway platform areas did not necessarily extend to the station building itself. In McKim's Pennsylvania Station, one went from

the Imperial Roman concourse to a waiting room rather like a conservatory, but when one reached platform level architecture was over and done with, and even planning seemed to have faded. At the Thirtieth Street Station in Philadelphia, the suburban commuter alights under platform shelters that are cleanly designed and mildly modernistic, only to make his way to a titanic, rather Fascist-looking, classical station building.

118. Le Corbusier, in *Vers une architecture* (G. Crès [Paris], 1923) was only one of the modernists who held up machine design and civil engineering as something to be emulated.

119. See Arthur Drexler, *The Architecture of Japan* (Museum of Modern Art, reprint of 1955 ed.).

120. See John Fitchen, *The Construction of Gothic Cathedrals: A Study of Medieval Vault Erection* (Clarendon Press [Oxford], 1961) or James H. Acland, *Medieval Structure: The Gothic Vault* (Toronto, 1972). The crossing of St. John the Divine, though built of solid masonry, shows alternate courses of some pier shafts omitted for bonding to other masonry if and when the crossing is completed.

121. See cross-sections of Prairie houses in *The Work of Frank Lloyd Wright* (the "Wendingen edition," 1923; reprinted Horizon, 1965). Wright discusses the materials of the Imperial Hotel in *An Autobiography* (Duell, Sloan and Pierce, 1943).

122. Geoffrey Scott, in *The Architecture of Humanism* (Scribner's, 1914; 1924), swats down the "fallacies" of the anti-classicists of his day one by one like so many flies. His attitude in general is "What if Renaissance architecture *is* superficial? It's the quality of the surface that counts." On this assumption he argues that an idealized representation of structure, structure used as a compositional device, is admissible, but the actual, working structure is often best concealed.

Art Deco; Modernistic

123. The skyscraper of the 1920's had little of the steel cage in its outer expression; rather, it looked like something modeled, carved, or extruded volcanically.

124. Of course there has been a rash lately of publications on these styles. Two books by Martin Battersby, *The Decorative Twenties* (Walker, 1969) and *The Decorative Thirties* (Walker, 1971) are probably the best summaries. See also Klaus Jürgen Sembach, *Style 1930* (Universe Books, 1971). From the period, see two books by Paul T. Frankl, *New Dimensions* (Brewer and Warren, 1928), and *Form and Re-Form* (Harper's, 1930; reprinted Hacker, 1972); unfortunately, the Hacker edition of the latter has chastened the layout somewhat. See also R. L. Leonard and C. A. Glassgold, eds., *Modern American Design* (Ives Washburn, 1930).

Ferment

125. See JSAH XXIV, 1 (March 1965), an issue devoted to "The Decade 1929–1939," and especially Robert A. M. Stern, "Relevance of the Decade," which summarizes the changes of 1927–28.

126. For early industrial design and designers, see Norman Bel Geddes, *Horizons* (Little Brown, 1932), Walter Dorwin Teague, *Design This Day* (Harcourt, Brace, 1940), and Raymond Loewy, *Never Leave Well Enough Alone* (Simon and Schuster, 1951).

127. See Henry-Russell Hitchcock, "Modern Architecture—A Memoir," JSAH XXVII, 4 (December 1968).

128. See Frank Lloyd Wright, *On Architecture*, ed. Frederick Gutheim (Duell, Sloan and Pierce, 1941), for long quotations from the 1928 series.

129. See Fig. 103 for the Harkness Memorial complex. Edgell mentions the grinding of the steps. Mizner regularly antiqued the decorative work of his houses, using hammers, air rifles, floggings with chains, broken bottles, acids, and soot.

130. Many such rooms can be seen in the Metropolitan Museum and its medieval branch The Cloisters, the Philadelphia Museum of Art, and in some mansions. Hearst imported, among other things, a Bavarian village and a Spanish monastery.

131. This is true of Andrew Jackson Downing, in *The Architecture of Country Houses* (Appleton, 1850) and William H. Ranlett, in *The Architect* (DeWitt and Davenport, 1847).

132. The consensus was that a return to Colonial was best; see Scully's scornful account of the editorials and correspondence in *Shingle Style.*

133. For modernist attitudes toward Eclecticism, see, for instance, Lewis Mumford, *Sticks and Stones*; Henry-Russell Hitchcock, *Modern Architecture*; Sheldon Cheney, *The New World Architecture* (Tudor, 1930); William Lescaze, *On Being an Architect* (G. P. Putnam's Sons, 1942); Elizabeth B. Mock, *If You Want to Build a House* (Museum of Modern Art, 1946); or Joseph Hudnut, *Architecture and the Spirit of Man* (Harvard, 1949).

134. H. Allen Brooks, in *The Prairie School*, awards the shelter magazines, going over to Eclecticism or Eclectic from the start, part of the blame for the demise of the Prairie School.

Survivals

135. Wills published extensively, mostly house plans and elevations, and practical advice for those about to build. See, for example, *Houses for Good Living* (Architectural Book Publishing Co., 1940; 1946) or *Planning Your Home Wisely* (Franklin Watts, 1946).

136. Given the cost of classical ornament, an American Renaissance architecture of any elaboration seems impossible, unless the creation of such ornament is given as made work to the unemployed or unless, as with James Bogardus' cast ironwork of the 1850s, it can be molded in some cheap material —these days presumably a highly durable plastic. Indeed, the villa design by Bayley in Fig. 151 calls for some modern techniques and materials. The walls were to be of concrete block, and some of the ornaments were to be stucco cast in rubber molds, with others molded in fiberglass. There was to be a Napoleonic bathroom with columns of lucite.

137. Venturi's own designs contain allusions to architectural forms of the past, although these are no more consistently used throughout a design than were the borrowings of the Queen Anne style.

Epilogue

138. For the older view of originality, see for example Bernard Berenson, "The Originality of Incompetence," in *Aesthetics and History* (Pantheon, 1948), and Dow, *American Renaissance*.

139. Of course, millions of such people still go to such churches in this way. For a while yet it will be possible to buy a Colonial steeple, prefabricated in aluminum and lowered onto a new church by a crane. The continuation of the Eclectic tradition is not here denied—nor is the sincerity of those who attend such churches in their Sunday best. But there has been a strong campaign to modernize Christianity in recent years, particularly its externals including architecture.

Index

Boldfaced numbers refer to illustrations or to captions, according to the context.

Sources of Illustrations

Numbers refer to figure numbers.